The Ultimate Jamaican Cookbook

111 Dishes From Jamaica To Cook Right Now

Slavka Bodic

Please sign up for free Balkan and Mediterranean recipes:
www.balkanfood.org

Introduction

Do you want to enjoy and celebrate the authentic Jamaican flavors by cooking some delicious and savory meals at home? Then you've found a perfect read for you! This cookbook is about to introduce you to some of the most popular Jamaican recipes and meals that 'you'll definitely adore, especially if you're a spice lover. Whether you've been to Jamaica or not, you can easily recreate its traditional cuisine at home with the help of this comprehensive cookbook. Jamaica is popular for its unique culture, amazing languages, and incredible food, so this book is one good way to come close to the flavorsome cuisine of this Caribbean island.

The Ultimate Jamaican Cookbook will introduce Jamaican cuisine and its culinary culture in a way that you may have never tried before. It brings you a variety of Jamaican recipes in one place. The cookbook is great for all those who always wanted to cook Jamaican food on their own without the help of a native Jamaican. Using this Jamaican cuisine cookbook, you can create a complete Jamaican menu of your own, or you can try all the special Jamaican recipes on different occasions as well. In this cookbook, you'll find popular Jamaican meals and ones that you might not have heard of formerly.

In these recipes, you'll discover some of the most commonly used Jamaican ingredients like jerk seasoning. Not only that, but you'll also learn how to make such seasonings and use them in different meals. The Jamaican cuisine has been comprised of various dishes from the Jamaican people and has been widely spread across the globe. There is a clear difference between taste and flavor in the food of various regions of Jamaica due to the vast ranges in culture and geological locations. And in this cookbook, you'll uncover all the recipes from different parts of Jamaica. Here's a summary of what you can gain in this cookbook:

- Insights about Jamaican cuisine
- Facts about Jamaica
- Jamaican breakfast recipes
- Snacks and appetizers
- Salads and sides
- Jamaican soups
- Main dishes
- Jamaican desserts and drinks

Let's try all these Jamaican Recipes and recreate a complete menu to celebrate the amazing Jamaican flavors and lovely aromas.

Table of Contents

Why Jamaican Cuisine?

Jamaican cuisine offer a mixture of flavors, cooking techniques, and spices influenced by African, Irish, Spanish, Amerindian, French, English, Portuguese, Indian, Chinese, and Middle Eastern people who live on the island. The cuisine is also impacted by the crops produced on the island or brought from Southeast Asia. All of those crops are now grown in Jamaica. A wide variety of tropical fruits, meats, and seafood are used in this cuisine.

Some Jamaican meals are prepared with variations brought to the island from other places of the world. These meals are modified to incorporate local food items and spices. Other recipes are unique or have a fusion that was developed locally over the years. Popular Jamaican dishes include fried dumplings, curry goat, ackee, saltfish, Jamaican patties, and various bread, pastries, and beverages.

In fact, Jamaican cuisine has spread to other parts of the world through emigrants during the 20th century. Jamaica is a great attraction for tourists; therefore, many people visit the country and take a part of its culture and cuisine along with them. This cuisine is comprised of various dishes of the native people and those brought by other people and disseminated across the globe. There's a clear difference between taste and flavor in the food of various regions of Jamaica due to the differences in cultural and geological locations. The major delights of this cuisine are as follows:

- Jamaican Cornmeal Porridge
- Authentic Caribbean Fried Johnny Cakes
- Jamaican Callaloo
- Jamaican Blue Draws
- Jamaican Egg Cake
- Jamaican Duckanoo Cakes
- Beef Soup
- Chicken Soup
- Corn Soup
- Cow Heel Soup
- Fish Tea
- Gun go Peas Soup

Among the desserts, there's a range of meals to look for, like mango cheesecake, upside-down cake, rum-soaked cake, and ice creams. The use of bananas, coconut, cornmeal, flour, and pineapple is common in this cuisine. Some popular Jamaican desserts include:

- Gizzada
- Grater cake
- Coconut Toto

Jamaica

Jamaica is one of the largest islands in the Caribbean Sea. It covers an area of 4,240 square miles, which makes it the third-largest island of the Caribbean and the Greater Antilles after Cuba and Hispaniola. It's located about 90 miles south of Cuba and 118 miles west of Hispaniola- the island which has the countries of the Dominican Republic and Haiti. There are British Overseas Territories of the Cayman Islands that encompass about 133 miles to the north-west of Jamaica.

Jamaica is the third-largest Caribbean island. The mountains like the Santa Cruz, Don Figueredo, and May Day mountains in the West, the John Crow and the Blue Mountains in the East, and the Dry Harbor Mountains in the center dominate most of this island. These mountains are surrounded by a coastal plain that's narrow. Jamaica is a country with only two cities, Kingston being the first city, the country's capital and business center, which is located on the south coast; and the second city is Montego Bay, which of the best cities in the Caribbean to visit as a tourist, which is located on the North coast. The seventh-largest natural harbor in the world- the Kingston harbor, is also present in Jamaica. Other major towns of Jamaica include:

- Portmore
- Spanish Town
- Savanna la Mar
- Mandeville
- Ocho ort Antonio

- Negril

Some of the major attractions of this country include the following:

- Negril Beach & the Negril Cliffs
- Rafting the Martha Brae River
- Dunn's River Falls
- Blue and John Crow Mountains National Park
- Port Antonio
- Doctor's Cave Beach, Montego Bay
- Blue Hole (Ocho Rios)
- Fort Charles
- The Hip Strip
- Green Grotto Caves

In retrospect, Jamaica has experienced all sorts of European influences in the past. It was ruled by the Spanish and the British, and those influences are reflected in the culture. Jamaica is the third most populous Anglophone country after the United States and Canada in the Americas; it also the fourth most populous Caribbean country.

Breakfast

Jamaican Green Banana Porridge

Preparation time: 10 minutes
Cook time: 15 minutes
Nutrition facts (per serving): 221 Cal (11g fat, 5g protein, 3g fiber)

This green banana porridge is a must in Jamaican cuisine. It's prepared mainly with evaporated milk and bananas, but then different side ingredients are added for flavor enhancement.

Ingredients (6 servings)

6 medium green bananas, peeled and sliced

1 ½ cups water

1 ½ cups evaporated milk

½ cup brown sugar

1 teaspoon vanilla extract

1 teaspoon ground nutmeg

1 teaspoon ground cinnamon

½ teaspoon ground allspice

½ teaspoon almond essence

¼ teaspoon salt

Preparation

Blend the bananas with spices and milk in a blender for 2 minutes. Mix the remaining porridge ingredients in a saucepan and cook for 15 minutes on a simmer with occasional stirring. Serve.

Jamaican Steamed Cabbage

Preparation time: 10 minutes
Cook time: 11 minutes
Nutrition facts (per serving): 236 Cal (17g fat, 19g protein, 2g fiber)

Jamaican steamed cabbage is a breakfast that you can serve every day with crispy bread and crispy bacon on the side.

Ingredients (2 servings)

½ medium head cabbage washed

1 medium carrot, washed

2 teaspoon olive oil or coconut oil

½ medium onion, chopped

2 garlic cloves, minced

¼ red bell pepper, chopped

2 sprigs of fresh thyme

2 green onions

½ teaspoon salt

¼ cup water

1 whole Scotch bonnet pepper

Preparation

Sauté the onion with salt, oil, bell pepper, garlic, and thyme in a skillet until onion is soft. Stir in carrots and cabbage, then sauté for 1 minute. Add the Scotch bonnet pepper and water. Cover and cook for 10 minutes with occasional stirring. Serve warm.

Bammy

Preparation time: 10 minutes
Cook time: 13 minutes
Nutrition facts (per serving): 308 Cal (10g fat, 14g protein, 0.4g fiber)

If you want something exotic and delicious on your breakfast menu, then nothing can taste better than these Jamaican Bammy pancakes.

Ingredients (4 servings)

2 pounds frozen cassava, grated
1 teaspoon salt
1 cup coconut milk
1 tablespoon sugar
3 tablespoon vegetable oil

Preparation

Add the grated cassava to cheesecloth, tie, and squeeze any excess liquid from it. Mix the cassava with sugar and salt in a suitable bowl. Divide the mixture into 8 flattened rounds. Set a skillet with oil over medium heat and sear the flattened rounds for 4 minutes per side. Transfer the rounds to coconut milk in a shallow tray for 20 minutes. Remove the pancakes from the milk and refry again for 5 minutes. Serve.

Jamaican Spice Bread

Preparation time: 5 minutes
Cook time: 1 hour
Nutrition facts (per serving): 423 Cal (17g fat, 23g protein, 1g fiber)

The Jamaican spice bread is loved by all due to its amazing taste and soft texture. This bread makes an irresistible serving for the table.

Ingredients (6 servings)
Batter
3 ¼ cups all-purpose flour
4 teaspoon baking powder
2 teaspoon ground cinnamon
1 teaspoon ground nutmeg
½ teaspoon ground allspice
1 pinch salt
1 egg
1 cup milk
⅓ cup beer
1 ¾ cups brown sugar
½ cup melted butter
1 teaspoon browning sauce
1 teaspoon vanilla extract
1 teaspoon lime juice
1 cup raisins

Glaze

½ cup brown sugar

½ cup water

Preparation

At 325 degrees F, preheat your oven. Grease 2 (8x4 inches) loaf pans. Mix the flour, salt, allspice, nutmeg, cinnamon, and baking powder in a suitable bowl. Stir in the egg, beer, milk, and 1 ¾ brown sugar, and then mix well. Add the lime juice, vanilla extract, browning sauce, and butter and then mix well. Fold in the raisins. Pour this batter into the loaf pans and bake for 1 hour. Mix ½ cup brown sugar and water in a small saucepan and cook to a boil on high heat. Reduce its heat, cook for 5 minutes, and then pour this glaze over the bread. Allow the bread to cool and serve.

Hard Do Bread

Preparation time: 10 minutes
Cook time: 30 minutes
Nutrition facts (per serving): 357 Cal (24g fat, 32g protein, 0g fiber)

Have you ever tried making the Jamaican Hard do bread at home? Well, here's a recipe to make some delicious do bread by yourself. Enjoy it with a delicious entree.

Ingredients (4 servings)

3 tablespoon white sugar
1 (¼ oz.) package dry yeast
¾ cup warm water
1 tablespoon vegetable oil
1 tablespoon margarine, melted
½ teaspoon salt
2¾ cups all-purpose flour

Preparation

Mix the sugar, warm water, and yeast in a suitable bowl and leave for 10 minutes. Stir in the flour, salt, margarine, and oil and then mix well. Knead this dough for 8 minutes and transfer to a greased bowl. Cover and leave the prepared dough for 1 hour. Punch the prepared dough and spread the prepared dough in a 9x5 inches loaf pan. Cover the prepared dough with a wet cloth and leave for 15 minutes. At 350 degrees F, preheat your oven. Bake the bread for 30 minutes and then allow it to cool. Slice and serve.

Ackee and Saltfish

Preparation time: 10 minutes
Cook time: 78 minutes
Nutrition facts (per serving): 136 Cal (4g fat, 14g protein, 2g fiber)

The famous Jamaican ackee and saltfish are here to make your breakfast special. You can always serve these with crispy bacon and fried eggs.

Ingredients (4 servings)

8 oz. salt cod
2 tablespoon neutral oil
2 tablespoon yellow onion, diced
2 tablespoon bell pepper, diced
½ Scotch bonnet chile, seeded, and minced
2 garlic cloves, minced
1 small tomato, cored and diced
1 scallion, sliced
2 tablespoon fresh thyme leaves, chopped
20-oz. can ackee
Salt and black pepper, to taste
Sliced avocado, for serving

Preparation

Rinse the cod with water and place in a suitable bowl. Pour fresh water on top, soak for 1 hour, cover, and refrigerate it overnight. Drain and transfer the cod to a saucepan and pour fresh water on top to cover. Boil the cod, reduce its heat, and cook for 40 minutes on medium heat. Drain and return the fish to the saucepan. Pour the fresh water on top and cook for another

20 minutes. Remove the fish skin and bones and then flake it into 1-inch pieces. Sauté the bell pepper, onion, garlic, and Scotch bonnet with oil in a skillet for 5 minutes. Add flakes to the salt cod and then sauté for 5 minutes. Stir in the thyme, scallion, and tomato and then cook for 5 minutes. Add the ackee and then cook for 3 minutes. Adjust the seasoning with black pepper and salt. Serve warm.

Corn Meal Porridge

Preparation time: 10 minutes
Cook time: 15 minutes
Nutrition facts (per serving): 402 Cal (23g fat, 19g protein, 3g fiber)

This cornmeal porridge is a classic Jamaican meal, great for breakfast and for side meals. You can try the porridge with a warmed tortilla and any other bread.

Ingredients (4 servings)

2 cups water
3 cups coconut milk
½ cinnamon stick
½ teaspoon salt
1 cup yellow cornmeal
1 teaspoon vanilla extract
½ teaspoon nutmeg
Coconut sugar, to taste
Brown sugar, to taste
½ cup sweetened condensed milk

Preparation

Boil 2 cups coconut milk with 2 cups water in a large saucepan. Add ½ stick cinnamon and cornmeal. Reduce its heat, mix well, and cook for 15 minutes. Stir in the condensed milk, nutmeg, vanilla extract, and coconut. Mix well and remove this pan from the heat. Serve.

Caribbean Fried Johnny Cakes

Preparation time: 15 minutes
Cook time: 3 minutes
Nutrition facts (per serving): 265 Cal (17g fat, 5g protein, 5.4g fiber)

It's about time to try some fried Johnny cakes on the breakfast menu and make it taste more diverse in flavors. In sum, it's a type of pancake. Serve warm with your favorite maple syrup on top.

Ingredients (2 servings)

2 ½ cups all-purpose flour

2 cups vegetable oil

¼ cup water

2 tablespoon butter

2 teaspoon sugar

1 ½ teaspoon baking powder

½ teaspoon salt

Preparation

Mix the flour with sugar, baking powder, and salt in a suitable bowl. Cut in the butter and then mix until crumbly. Pour in the water and then mix until smooth. Knead this dough, cover, and leave for 30 minutes. Divide the prepared dough into small balls and keep them aside. Pour 3 cups of oil into a cooking pan and heat it. Deep fry the prepared dough balls for 3 minutes until golden brown. Transfer the balls to a plate with a slotted spoon. Serve warm.

Jamaican Callaloo

Preparation time: 15 minutes
Cook time: 10 minutes
Nutrition facts (per serving): 242 Cal (6g fat, 9g protein, 10g fiber)

The Jamaican callaloo is a delicious morning meal you can try every day; it's best to serve with bread. You can try different herb toppings as well.

Ingredients (4 servings)
4 cups callaloo, chopped
1 tablespoon olive oil
1 small onion, chopped
2 garlic cloves, minced
2 green onions, chopped
2 sprigs thyme
1 medium tomato, chopped
Salt, to taste
1 Scotch bonnet pepper, whole
2 tablespoon water

Preparation
Remove the calloo's outer old leaves and remove the membrane of each stalk. Transfer the callaloo to a large bowl, pour 2 teaspoon water, and then leave for 30 minutes. Drain and rinse the callaloo. Sauté the onion, garlic, spring onion, thyme, tomato, and bonnet pepper with oil in a skillet until soft. Stir in the water and the callaloo and then cook for 10 minutes on low heat. Serve warm.

Jamaican Blue Draws

Preparation time: 15 minutes
Cook time: 60 minutes
Nutrition facts (per serving): 213 Cal (20g fat, 12g protein, 7g fiber)

This dish is prepared with banana leaves, a banana, and sweet potato filling, which make them an excellent breakfast serving.

Ingredients (4 servings)
2 cups cornmeal
1 cup gluten-free flour
1 ½ cups cane sugar
½ teaspoon cinnamon
¼ teaspoon nutmeg
½ teaspoon salt
2 cups coconut milk
2 fingers green bananas, peeled and chopped
1 medium sweet potato, peeled and chopped
2 teaspoon vanilla
1 cup grated coconut
⅓ cup raisins
Fresh banana leaves
Baker's twine, for tying

Preparation
Cut the banana leaf into equal rectangular pieces. Parboil the leaves in boil water until wilted, drain, and transfer to a plate. Mix the cornmeal with salt, nutmeg, cinnamon, sugar, and flour in a suitable bowl. Blend the vanilla,

sweet potato, green banana, and coconut milk in a food processor. Stir in the flour mixture and mix well. Fold in the raisins and the coconut. Mix well and divide the banana batter at the center of each rectangle piece. Fold the leaves, cover the filling, and tie the leaves to secure. Place the packs in a cooking pot filled with water. Cook the water to a boil, reduce its heat, and cook for 1 hour. Remove the leave packs using a pair of tongs and serve.

Jamaican Egg Cake

Preparation time: 10 minutes
Cook time: 35 minutes
Nutrition facts (per serving): 121 Cal (10g fat, 12g protein, 2g fiber)

It's almost as if the Jamaican menu is incomplete without this classic. These egg cakes are great to serve with toasted bread.

Ingredients (2 servings)
2 eggs
½ cup cake flour
3 tablespoon 1 teaspoon castor sugar
¾ teaspoon olive oil
Warm water

Preparation
At 350 degrees F, preheat your oven. Add water to cooking pan and set a suitable glass bowl in it. Mix the sugar and the eggs in this mixture and continue mixing for 15 minutes on this heat until fluffy. Remove the egg mixture from the heat and stir in the oil and the flour. Mix well and divide the mixture into a greased muffin tray. Bake the batter for 20 minutes in the oven. Allow the muffins to cool and serve.

Jamaican Duckanoo Cakes

Preparation time: 15 minutes
Cook time: 10 minutes
Nutrition facts (per serving): 142 Cal (4g fat, 12g protein, 1g fiber)

Duckanoo cakes are another Jamaican morning cake recipe that you can try in breakfast as well. Due to its simple and quick recipe, you can easily prepare it at home.

Ingredients (4 servings)

2 oz. of corn flour

3 ½ oz. of wheat flour

1 teaspoon of yeast

5 oz. of grated coconut

1 tablespoon of natural vanilla extract

8 ½ oz. of milk

1 ½ oz. of raisins

½ oz. of butter

1 oz. of muscovado sugar

½ a teaspoon of cinnamon powder

½ a teaspoon of nutmeg powder

Preparation

At 360 degrees F, preheat your oven. Mix the flour with the coconut and the yeast in a suitable bowl. Stir in the milk and the vanilla and then mix evenly. Add the cinnamon, nutmeg, raisins, sugar, 1 tablespoon cold water, and melted butter and then mix well. Knead this dough and divide the prepared dough into a small ball. Place these balls on a baking sheet with parchment paper. Bake the bake balls until golden brown. Serve.

Appetizers and Snacks

Jamaican Meat Pie Footballs

Preparation time: 10 minutes
Cook time: 36 minutes
Nutrition facts (per serving): 379 Cal (18g fat, 21g protein, 6g fiber)

This beef-filled football recipe has unique flavors due to its rich mix of beef with veggies and spices in its filling. Serve warm with your favorite dip on the side.

Ingredients (6 servings)
2 teaspoon fresh thyme leaves
6 scallions, chopped
2 garlic cloves, chopped
1 Scotch bonnet chile, seeds removed and chopped
½ green bell pepper, stemmed, seeded and chopped
8 oz. ground beef
1 ½ teaspoon Jamaican curry powder
¼ teaspoon ground allspice
2 tablespoon vegetable oil
Salt and black pepper, to taste
2 (17-oz.) packages puff pastry (4 sheets)
1 large egg, beaten
Barbecue sauce, chutney or ranch dressing, for serving

Preparation
At 400 degrees F, preheat your oven. Layer 2 baking sheets with wax paper. Blend the bell pepper, bonnet chile, garlic, scallions, and thyme in a food processor. Sauté the beef with oil in a stock for 2 minutes until brown. Stir

in the allspice, curry powder, and pepper mixture and then cook for 5 minutes. Remove it from the heat and add the oil, black pepper, and salt. Mix well and keep it aside. Roll each puff pastry into ⅛-inch-thick sheet. Cut 8 ovals from each sheet and add a tablespoon of beef mixture at the center of each oval. Fold the prepared dough in half, crimp, and brush the wraps with the egg mixture. Place the patties in a baking sheet. Use the leftover dough to cut strips and make cross patterns over the patties. Bake the patties for 30 minutes and then serve warm.

Spiced Jamaican Rolls (Bulla)

Preparation time: 10 minutes
Cook time: 25 minutes
Nutrition facts (per serving): 278 Cal (10g fat, 34g protein, 2g fiber)

If you can't think of anything delicious and savory to serve, then try this avocado stuff roll because it has great taste and texture for the table.

Ingredients (4 servings)

3 ½ oz. unsalted butter, chopped
1 tablespoon vanilla extract
1¾ cups firmly packed brown sugar
1 ½ inch piece ginger, peeled, grated
4⅔ cups plain flour
1 tablespoon baking powder
2 teaspoon baking soda
½ teaspoon ground cinnamon
Sliced avocado, to serve

Preparation

At 360 degrees f, preheat your oven. Mix the butter, 7 cups water, 2 teaspoon salt, ginger, sugar, and vanilla in a saucepan. Next, cook on low heat for 5 minutes. Stir in the baking soda, cinnamon, baking powder, and flour and then mix well. Pour in the sugar mixture and mix well. Knead for 5 minutes and then roll into 1 inch thick sheet. Cut 3–4-inch rounds. Place these rounds on a baking sheet, lined with parchment paper. Bake the rounds for 25 minutes. Top them with avocado slices. Serve.

Jamaican Jerk Burrito

Preparation time: 5 minutes
Cook time: 13 minutes
Nutrition facts (per serving): 386 Cal (11g fat, 27g protein, 4g fiber)

Simple and easy to make, this jerk burrito recipe is a must to try on this menu. Serve them with your favorite tomato sauce.

Ingredients (8 servings)

¾ cup Jamaican jerk marinade
5 tablespoon lime juice
2 garlic cloves, minced
1 pinch black pepper
2 cups extra-firm tofu, pressed and cubed
Cooking spray
2 cups jicama, diced
1 cup pineapple, diced
2 cups prepared rice
1 (15 oz.) can black beans, drained

Burritos

8 (8 inches) low-fat flour tortilla
½ cup Monterey Jack cheese, shredded
½ cup salsa
½ cup sour cream

Preparation

Mix the black pepper, ½ cup marinade, garlic, and ¼ cup lime juice in a suitable bowl. Stir in the tofu, mix well to coat, cover, and refrigerate for 30 minutes. Sear the tofu in a greased skillet for 4 minutes per side. Transfer this tofu to a plate and add the rest of the ingredients to the skillet. Cook for 3 minutes on medium heat. Stir in the tofu and cook for about 2 minutes. Divide the tofu mixture on top of each tortilla and top it with cheese, salsa, and sour cream. Finally, roll the tortillas into burritos. Serve.

Jerk Spiced Nuts

Preparation time: 15 minutes
Cook time: 22 minutes
Nutrition facts (per serving): 199 Cal (8g fat, 4g protein, 1g fiber)

These jerk spiced nuts are here to complete your Jamaican menu. They can be served on all special occasions and festive celebrations.

Ingredients (6 servings)

1 (20 oz.) bag mixed nuts

2 egg whites

2 teaspoons garlic powder

2 teaspoon cayenne pepper

1 teaspoon dried parsley

1 tablespoon brown sugar

1 teaspoon salt

½ teaspoon allspice

½ teaspoon pepper

¾ teaspoon crushed red pepper

½ teaspoon nutmeg

¼ teaspoon cinnamon

Preparation

At 350 degrees F, preheat your oven. Layer a baking sheet with cooking spray. Beat the egg whites in a suitable bowl, add the spices, and mix well. Stir in the nuts and mix well. Spread the nuts on the prepared baking sheet and bake for 22 minutes. Lastly, toss them once cooked halfway through. Serve.

Sweet Potato Pudding

Preparation time: 10 minutes
Cook time: 60 minutes
Nutrition facts (per serving): 141 Cal (4g fat, 12g protein, 1.1g fiber)

Here comes a Jamaican side meal that's beloved by all. The sweet potato pudding pairs well with a variety of entrées.

Ingredients (4 servings)

2 lbs. sweet potato, grated
¼ lb. yellow yam, grated
½ cup flour
1 teaspoon baking powder
¼ cup raisins
¼ teaspoon nutmeg, grated
½ lb. brown sugar
1 teaspoon vanilla flavoring
4 cups coconut milk
½ teaspoon salt
1½ oz. butter

Preparation

Add the raisins, yam, potato, baking powder, and flour in a saucepan. Stir in the butter, coconut milk, nutmeg, vanilla, and brown sugar. Mix well until smooth. Grease a baking pan with butter and pour the sweet potato mixture into the pan. Allow it to set for 20 minutes. At 350 degrees F, preheat your oven. Bake the pudding for 40 minutes. Check the pudding and bake more until golden brown. Slice and serve.

Jamaican Beef Patties

Preparation time: 15 minutes
Cook time: 42 minutes
Nutrition facts (per serving): 196 Cal (6g fat, 13g protein, 2g fiber)

These beef patties are popular Jamaican snacks that are enjoyed all over the world. They deliver a delightful mix of beef filling inside flour and turmeric wraps.

Ingredients (4 servings)

2 lbs. ground beef
2 stalks scallions, chopped
1 large onion, chopped
1½ cups breadcrumbs
2 stalks thyme, chopped
1 teaspoon sugar
1 teaspoon salt
1 Scotch bonnet pepper, chopped and seeded
1 cup beef stock

Pie crust

2 lbs. self-rising flour
1 cup beef suet
1 tablespoon Ground turmeric
1 stick margarine
1-pint cold water

Preparation

Mix the flour, water, margarine, and turmeric in a suitable bowl until smooth. Roll this dough over the working surface into a ⅛-inch-thick sheet. Cut the prepared dough into circles using a 3-inch cookie cutter. Sauté the beef in a greased skillet until brown. Stir in the onions, scallions, sugar, salt, bonnet pepper, and thyme. Next, sauté for 20 minutes. Stir in the breadcrumbs, cook for 7 minutes, and mix well. Divide the filling at the center of the prepared dough rounds and fold each round in half. Pinch the edges to seal the patties and place them in a baking sheet. Finally, bake for 35 minutes in the oven. Serve warm.

Jamaican Spiced Potato Wedges

Preparation time: 5 minutes
Cook time: 35 minutes
Nutrition facts (per serving): 231 Cal (11g fat, 8g protein, 0.3g fiber)

These spiced potato wedges make a great serving if you're seeking a quick snack. Serve these wedges with some ketchup or onion dip.

Ingredients (10 servings)

5 lbs. Desirée potatoes
4 tablespoon olive oil
3 tablespoon Jamaican jerk seasoning
9 ½ oz. tub soured cream, to serve
1 lime, cut into wedges, to garnish

Preparation

At 360 degrees f, preheat your oven. Wash and pat dry the potatoes and then cut them into thin wedges. Toss the potato wedges with oil and jerk seasoning in a suitable bowl. Spread them onto 2 toasting pans and bake for 35 minutes until crispy. Toss the potatoes once cooked halfway through. Serve with lime wedges and sour cream.

Jamaican Saltfish Fritters

Preparation time: 15 minutes
Cook time: 4 minutes
Nutrition facts (per serving): 103 Cal (12g fat, 13g protein, 1.4g fiber)

If you haven't tried the Jamaican saltfish fritters before, then here comes a simple and easy to cook recipe that you can easily prepare and cook at home in no time with minimum efforts.

Ingredients (2 servings)

½ lb. boneless salted cod fish
2 teaspoon baking powder
1 cup all-purpose flour
1 teaspoon granulated garlic
½ teaspoon smoked paprika
½ teaspoon sugar
½ medium onion, diced
½ teaspoon Scotch bonnet pepper, minced
3 tablespoon parsley, minced
1 teaspoon fresh thyme, minced
2 tablespoon bell pepper, minced
1 large egg
½ cup milk
Black pepper, to taste
3 cups vegetable oil for frying

Preparation

Soak the fish in water overnight, drain, and shred in a food processor. Mix the rest of the fish ingredients in a suitable bowl until smooth. Fold in the grated fish. Preheat the cooking oil in a deep pan at 350 degrees F. Drop a spoonful of batter into the hot oil one after the other and cook for 4 minutes until golden brown. Transfer the fritters to a plate using a slotted spoon. Serve.

Jamaican Fried Ripe Plantains

Preparation time: 15 minutes
Cook time: 10 minutes
Nutrition facts (per serving): 175 Cal (9g fat, 1g protein, 2g fiber)

Have you ever tried these fried ripe plantains? Well, here's a recipe to cook them by yourself with easy-to-follow ingredients.

Ingredients (4 servings)

4 firm, ripe plantains
Vegetable oil for deep frying
1 tablespoon cinnamon
1 tablespoon vanilla extract

Preparation

Slice the plantains and keep them on a plate. Add the oil to a deep-frying pan and heat to 350 degrees F. Deep fry the plantains until golden brown. Transfer the plantains to a plate using a slotted spoon. Drizzle cinnamon and vanilla on top. Serve.

Caribbean Dumpling

Preparation time: 15 minutes
Cook time: 15 minutes
Nutrition facts (per serving): 158 Cal (12g fat, 7g protein, 2g fiber)

These simple, quick and easy to make Caribbean dumplings have no parallel. If you have some flour, and cornmeal along with some other ingredients at home, then you can prepare them in no time.

Ingredients (4 servings)
Jamaican Festival
2 ¼ cups flour
¾ cup cornmeal
2 teaspoon baking powder
¾ teaspoon salt
3 tablespoon sugar
3 tablespoon soft butter
1 cup milk
1 teaspoon grated nutmeg spice
Oil for deep-frying

Mango Coleslaw
1 cup purple cabbage, sliced
4 cups cabbage, sliced
2 cups mango, sliced
½ medium onion, sliced
½ red bell pepper, sliced
2 cups carrots, sliced

Dressing

½ tablespoon mustard

¼ tablespoon honey

½ cup Non-Fat Greek yogurt

½ cup Low Fat mayonnaise

1 teaspoon salt

½ teaspoon black pepper

1 lemon juice

1 teaspoon sriracha

Preparation

Mix the onions with carrots, red bell pepper, mango, and cabbage in a large bowl. Stir in the honey, lemon juice, mustard, black pepper, salt, mayonnaise, and yogurt. Next, t mix well. Mix the butter with salt, nutmeg, cornmeal, baking powder, and flour in a large bowl. Pour in the milk and mix well until smooth. Knead the prepared dough for 1 minute. Divide the prepared dough into 14 equal pieces. Shape each dough pieces into a sausage shape. Cut a slit on top of the dumplings and deep fry them in hot cooking oil at 350 degrees F, until golden brown. Transfer the prepared dumplings to a plate and serve with mango coleslaw. Enjoy.

Jamaican Coconut Tart (Gizzada)

Preparation time: 10 minutes
Cook time: 32 minutes
Nutrition facts (per serving): 174 Cal (3g fat, 1g protein, 3g fiber)

Have you tried the famous coconut tart? If you haven't, now is the time to cook these delicious tarts at home using simple and healthy ingredients.

Ingredients (4 servings)
Crust
1 ⅔ cup flour
¼ cup sugar
½ cup butter
2 egg yolks
6 teaspoon cold water

Filling
1 cup brown sugar
2 eggs
½ teaspoon pure vanilla extract
⅛ teaspoon grated nutmeg
2 cups coconut flakes
2 tablespoon melted butter
Pinch of salt

Preparation
Mix the flour with sugar in a small bowl. Cut in the flour and mix until crumbly. Beat in the egg yolks, pour water, and then mix until smooth.

Wrap the prepared dough in a plastic wrap and refrigerate for ½ hour. At 350 degrees F, preheat your oven. Spread the prepared dough into a ⅛-inch-thick sheet. Cut the sheet using a 4 ½ inch cookie cutter into circles. Place one circle into each muffin cups of a muffin tray. Press the prepared dough and bake these shells for 7 minutes. Meanwhile, beat the eggs with brown sugar, vanilla, nutmeg, coconut, butter, and salt in a suitable bowl. Divide the filling into the shells and bake for 25 minutes. Allow them to cool and serve.

Cornmeal Fritters

Preparation time: 10 minutes
Cook time: 20 minutes
Nutrition facts (per serving): 191 Cal (17g fat, 8g protein, 2g fiber)

Here are simple Jamaican cornmeal fritters made out of cornmeal, milk and flour. Serve these fritters with your favorite sauce.

Ingredients (2 servings)
½ cup cornmeal
1 cup milk
2 tablespoons margarine
Salt, to taste
1 teaspoon baking powder
1 tablespoon sugar
2 drops vanilla essence
½ cup refined flour
1 egg, beaten
Oil to deep fry

Preparation
Mix the flour with cornmeal in a suitable bowl. Stir in the baking powder, rub, salt, and margarine, and then mix until crumbly. Stir in the milk, vanilla essence, sugar, and egg and then mix until smooth. Set a deep-frying pan with oil over medium-high heat. Drop the batter into the hot oil spoon by spoon and cook until golden brown. Transfer them to a plate lined with a paper towel. Serve.

Caribbean Sweet Potato Patties

Preparation time: 10 minutes
Cook time: 80 minutes
Nutrition facts (per serving): 203 Cal (4g fat, 9g protein, 1g fiber)

Make these Jamaican sweet potato patties in no time and enjoy them with some garnish on top. Adding a drizzle of sesame seeds on top makes them super tasty.

Ingredients (2 servings)

1 large sweet potato, peeled and cubed
2 tablespoon olive oil
½ teaspoon ground allspice
½ teaspoon ground cumin
¼ teaspoon dried chili flakes
½ teaspoon dried thyme
1 whole bulb garlic, outer leaves removed
2 Scotch bonnet chillies, chopped
3 spring onions, chopped
Salt and black pepper, to taste
1 handful of fresh coriander leaves, chopped
Zest of ½ a lime
Few sprigs of fresh thyme leaves

Preparation

At 420 degrees F, preheat your oven. Toss the sweet potato cubes with cumin, allspice, thyme, black pepper, salt, chili flakes, and oil on a baking sheet. Roast the sweet potato for 20 minutes. Transfer the sweet potatoes to a bowl. Spread the garlic on a baking sheet and roast for 30-40 minutes. Mash the sweet potatoes in a suitable bowl. Peel and add the roasted garlic to the sweet potatoes. Mash and mix well. Sauté the onions and bonnets with oil in a skillet until soft. Stir in the mashed potatoes, lime zest, and coriander. Mix well and keep it aside. Make 4 patties from this mixture. Place these patties on a baking sheet and bake for 5-10 minutes until golden brown. Serve.

Fry Jacks Belize

Preparation time: 15 minutes
Cook time: 10 minutes
Nutrition facts (per serving): 167 Cal (5g fat, 3g protein, 3g fiber)

The famous fry jacks Belize with tomato sauce on the side are on the Jamaican menu. Make them at home with these healthy ingredients and enjoy.

Ingredients (4 servings)

2 cups flour
2 teaspoon baking powder
¾ teaspoon salt
2 tablespoon shortening
1 tablespoon sugar
¾ cup whole milk
Oil for deep-frying

Preparation

Mix the flour with salt, baking powder, and sugar in a large bowl. Cut in the shortening and then mix until crumbly. Pour in the milk, mix well, and knead the prepared dough for 1 minute. Divide this prepared dough into 6 pieces. Roll out each dough pieces into a circle. Cut the circle in half and then make a slit on top. Deep fry the prepared dough pieces in hot oil for 5 minutes until golden brown. Transfer the bread pieces to a plate using a slotted spoon. Enjoy with refried beans, cheese, butter, and honey.

Candied Sweet Potatoes

Preparation time: 10 minutes
Cook time: 40 minutes
Nutrition facts (per serving): 213 Cal (11g fat, 5g protein, 1g fiber)

Best to serve as a healthy side meal, these Jamaican candied sweet potatoes are loaded with nutrients and flavors.

Ingredients (8 servings)

4 lbs. sweet potatoes
2 tablespoon butter
1 cup brown sugar, packed
1 teaspoon salt
1 tablespoon cinnamon
½ cup water

Preparation

Peel and cut the potatoes into 1-inch thick slices. Pat dry the sweet potatoes with a paper towel. Place the prepared sweet potatoes in a baking dish. At 300 degrees F, bake the sweet potatoes until soft. Mix the sugar with melted butter, cinnamon, salt, and water in a saucepan and cook on low heat until it thickens. Pour this sauce over the sweet potatoes. Serve.

Salads

Jamaican Garden Salad

Preparation time: 10 minutes
Nutrition facts (per serving): 261 Cal (3g fat, 5g protein, 1g fiber)

The Jamaican garden salad is a great delight that you can easily prepare at home. The salad is fairly easy to make and doesn't require any complicated cooking techniques.

Ingredients (4 servings)

4 cups cabbage, shredded

4 carrots, shredded

1 green pepper, sliced

1 tomato, cut into 8 wedges

½ English cucumber, peel on and sliced

¼ cup Thousand Island dressing

Preparation

Toss the cabbage with the cucumber and the rest of the ingredients in a salad bowl. Serve.

Jamaican Cabbage Salad

Preparation time: 15 minutes
Nutrition facts (per serving): 149 Cal (1g fat, 9g protein, 0.1g fiber)

Cabbage salad is everyone's favorite go-to meal. It's full of calories and good taste. There's a healthy taste of cabbage with cucumber, carrots, and celery.

Ingredients (4 servings)
1 head green cabbage, julienned
4 medium carrots, julienned
6 stalks celery, julienned
1 large cucumber, julienned
½ cup sugar
½ cup vinegar
1 splash olive oil
4 cups boiling water

Preparation
Toss the cabbage with the carrots and the rest of the veggies in a large bowl. Pour boiling water on top and leave for 20 minutes. Drain and transfer the veggies to a salad bowl. Stir in the rest of the ingredients. Mix well and serve.

Caribbean-Style Sofrito

Preparation time: 10 minutes
Nutrition facts (per serving): 16 Cal (1g fat, 1g protein, 1g fiber)

Let's make some sofrito with these simple ingredients. Mix them together and then cook to achieve a great combination of flavors.

Ingredients (6 servings)

2 green bell peppers, cubed

2 red bell peppers, cubed

1 orange bell pepper, cubed

1 yellow bell pepper, cubed

10 tomatoes, cored and chopped

1 bunch green onions, chopped

1½ bunches fresh cilantro leaves, chopped

6 fresh tomatillos, husks removed

1 cup garlic, chopped

Preparation

Blend the bell peppers in a food processor. Add the garlic, tomatillos, cilantro, green onions, and tomatoes. Finally, blend until chunky. Serve.

Jamaican Confetti Rice Salad

Preparation time: 10 minutes
Nutrition facts (per serving): 271 Cal (17g fat, 16g protein, 2g fiber)

If you haven't tried the famous confetti rice salad yet, then here comes a simple and easy to cook recipe that you can recreate at home in no time with minimum efforts.

Ingredients (4 servings)
2 cups white long-grain rice
1 red capsicum, diced
1 green capsicum, diced
½ pineapple, peeled, cored and diced
½ cup shredded coconut, toasted
2 green onions, sliced
⅓ cup fresh coriander, chopped
1 jalapeno pepper, halved, seeded, and sliced

Jerk Dressing
2 tablespoon lime juice
2 tablespoon olive oil
¾ inch piece fresh ginger, grated
2 teaspoons brown sugar
1 teaspoon ground cumin
½ teaspoon ground cinnamon
½ teaspoon dried thyme
¼ teaspoon ground allspice

Preparation

Cook the rice as per the package's instructions, rinse, and drain. Mix the cooked rice with the rest of the ingredients in a salad bowl. Serve.

Jamaican Chicken Salad

Preparation time: 10 minutes
Nutrition facts (per serving): 244 Cal (12g fat, 15g protein, 1g fiber)

This chicken salad has a delightful mix of cheese, chicken, carrots, and cucumbers. Serve this salad with your favorite entree.

Ingredients (4 servings)

1 (10 oz.) pkg. cooked chicken breast strips

1 teaspoon jerk seasoning mix

1 ½ cups cheddar jack cheese, shredded

¾ cup carrots, julienned

½ cup cucumber, diced

¼ cup almonds, toasted and sliced

¼ cup light mayonnaise

2 tablespoon seasoned rice vinegar

Salad greens, to serve

Preparation

Toss the chicken with the seasoning and the rest of the ingredients in a salad bowl. Serve.

Chicken Avocado Salad

Preparation time: 15 minutes
Cook time: 14 minutes
Nutrition facts (per serving): 144 Cal (17g fat, 16g protein, 1g fiber)

The avocado chicken salad is here to make your dinner menu a little more delicious and nourishing. This salad has a unique blend of cucumber, pineapple, avocados, and bell peppers.

Ingredients (6 servings)
Jamaican Jerk Chicken
2 pounds boneless chicken thighs
4 habanero peppers, seeded
2 tablespoon fresh thyme leaves
½ small red onion
1 tablespoon ginger, grated
4 garlic cloves
3 tablespoon soy sauce
2 tablespoon lime juice
2 tablespoon brown sugar
2 teaspoon ground allspice
1 teaspoon cinnamon
½ teaspoon nutmeg
1 teaspoon salt
½ teaspoon black pepper

Salad

2 heads romaine lettuce, chopped

2 large red bell peppers, cut into rings

2 ripe avocados, peeled and sliced

1 English cucumber, sliced

½ ripe pineapple, cut into chunks

1 bottle honey mustard dressing

Preparation

Place the chicken on the working surface and blend the rest of its seasoning ingredients in a blender. Pour this prepared marinade over the chicken and rub well. Cover and marinate for 1 hour in the refrigerator. Set a grill over medium-high heat and grill the chicken for 5 minutes per side. Slice the grilled chicken and keep it side. Grill the red pepper rings for 2 minutes per side. Toss the grilled pepper with the avocado slices, pineapple, and cucumbers. Add this salad on top of lettuce leaves on a plate. Place the grilled chicken on top and serve with dressing on top.

Caribbean Salad with Honey Dressing

Preparation time: 15 minutes
Nutrition facts (per serving): 226 Cal (3g fat, 13g protein, 0.1g fiber)

The appetizing and savory Caribbean salad offers a great addition to your Jamaican menu, and it looks spectacular when served at the table.

Ingredients (8 servings)
Salad
8 cups salad greens
2 cups pineapple, cubed
2 cups mandarin orange segments
½ cup dried cranberries
½ cup cilantro chopped
1 bunch green onions, sliced
4 teaspoon chia seeds
4 teaspoon sesame seeds
2 cups black beans

Honey Lime Dressing
2 tablespoon honey
2 tablespoon apple cider vinegar
1 tablespoon lime juice
¼ cup canola oil
1 tablespoon onion, diced
Pinch of salt

Preparation

Toss the greens with the pineapple and the rest of the ingredients in a salad bowl. Serve.

Chicken Jicama Salad

Preparation time: 10 minutes
Cook time: 40 minutes
Nutrition facts (per serving): 123 Cal (5g fat, 4g protein, 1g fiber)

Here comes a nutritious meal made with all healthy ingredients. Serve this salad with your favorite entree.

Ingredients (6 servings)
Jerk Rub
10 Scotch bonnet chile peppers, chopped
¼ cup fresh basil
¼ cup fresh thyme
¼ cup fresh ginger, minced
¼ cup yellow mustard
4 garlic cloves, chopped
3 scallions, chopped
2 tablespoon dried rosemary, chopped
2 tablespoon fresh parsley, chopped
2 tablespoon brown mustard seeds
2 tablespoon each orange juice and white vinegar
1 teaspoon ground allspice
1 teaspoon salt and 1 teaspoon black pepper
¼ teaspoon ground cloves
¼ teaspoon grated nutmeg
Lime juice
6 chicken thighs, skin removed

Dressing

1 garlic clove, chopped

Coarse salt, to taste

2 tablespoon lime juice

Caribbean hot sauce

2 tablespoon vegetable oil

Salad

1 cup jicama, julienned

½ cup strips red and yellow bell pepper, julienned

2 tomatoes, cut into wedges

1 avocado, sliced

1 teaspoon lime peel, grated

Minced fresh chiles

Minced fresh cilantro

1 head Boston lettuce, leaves separated

Preparation

Mix all the jerk rub ingredients in a food processor. Rub the jerk seasoning over the chicken and cut the slits on top. Grill the chicken for 40 minutes and flip once cooked halfway through. Allow the cooked chicken to cool and cut into slices. Mix the rest of the salad ingredients in a salad bowl. Top the salad with the grilled chicken. Serve.

Grilled Pineapple Salad

Preparation time: 10 minutes
Cook time: 4 minutes
Nutrition facts (per serving): 253 Cal (18g g fat, 9g protein, 3g fiber)

The famous grilled pineapple salad is a wonderful side meal. Try making it at home with these healthy ingredients and enjoy.

Ingredients (4 servings)

½ fresh pineapple, peeled, cored, and cut into rings
6 oz. pineapple juice
1 tablespoon minced fresh ginger
2 teaspoon simple jerk seasoning
1 head red leaf lettuce, chopped
2 cups mini sweet peppers, sliced
¾ cup unsweetened coconut flakes

Preparation

Set a grill over medium-high heat and grease its grates with oil. Grill pineapple rings 2 minutes per side, covered. Cut the grilled rings into bite-sized chunks. Toss the rest of the ingredients in a salad bowl. Add the pineapple, mix well, and serve.

Grilled Pork Tenderloin Salad

Preparation time: 10 minutes
Cook time: 20 minutes
Nutrition facts (per serving): 243 Cal (13g fat, 24g protein, 0.2g fiber)

This grilled pork tenderloin salad is a Jamaican specialty. Plus, it's served on all special occasions. It's prepared using a nice mix of pork with greens, pineapple, and papaya.

Ingredients (4 servings)
Dressing
2 tablespoon 2 teaspoon dried thyme leaves
2 tablespoon fresh lime juice
1 tablespoon olive oil
1 tablespoon fresh ginger, minced
2 teaspoon brown sugar
½ teaspoon salt
½ teaspoon ground allspice
½ teaspoon ground cinnamon
¼ teaspoon black pepper
¼ teaspoon ground nutmeg
1 garlic clove, minced

Salad
1 (1-pound) pork tenderloin
Cooking spray
4 cups salad greens
2 cups peeled fresh pineapple, chopped
1 cup papaya, chopped

Preparation

Set up a grill over medium heat. Blend the salad dressing ingredients in a food processor until smooth. Slice the pork lengthwise, open its halves, and rub the dressing over the pork. Grill this pork for 10 minutes per side. Cut the grilled pork into ¼ inch thick slices. Mix this pork with the remaining dressing in a large bowl. Serve the pork, pineapple, and papaya over a bed of greens on four plates. Enjoy.

Corn and Black Bean Salad

Preparation time: 10 minutes
Nutrition facts (per serving): 252 Cal (11g fat, 17g protein, 5g fiber)

The corn and black bean salad is one delicious way to complete your Jamaican menu; here's a recipe for a tasty meal.

Ingredients (4 servings)

1 (28 oz.) bag frozen corn thawed
1 red bell pepper, seeded and diced
1 green bell pepper, seeded and diced
1 16 oz. can of black beans rinsed and drained
1 cup celery diced
2 cups tomatoes, peeled and chopped
1 cup fresh cilantro, chopped
1 cup red onion diced
1 teaspoon cumin
1 teaspoon chili powder
½ cup raspberry vinaigrette
½ cup balsamic vinaigrette

Preparation

Toss the tomatoes with the celery and the rest of the ingredients in a salad bowl. Serve.

Jerk Shrimp Pineapple Salad

Preparation time: 10 minutes
Cook time: 18 minutes
Nutrition facts (per serving): 280 Cal (15g fat, 12g protein, 2g fiber)

This shrimp pineapple salad is made primarily from grilled shrimp and a mix of pineapple with veggies. Serve it with your favorite entree.

Ingredients (8 servings)

1 cup unsweetened pineapple juice
1 teaspoon lime zest, grated
3 tablespoon lime juice
1 tablespoon canola oil
2 garlic cloves, chopped
½ teaspoon dried thyme
½ teaspoon dried oregano
¼ teaspoon ground cinnamon
¼ teaspoon ground allspice
2 tablespoon Jamaican jerk sauce
20 large shrimp, peeled and deveined
3 cups cooked white rice
1 16-oz. can black beans, rinsed
Salt and black pepper, to taste
2 cups fresh pineapple chunks
6 thick scallions, trimmed and chopped
1 head Boston lettuce, washed, dried and torn
Lime slices for garnish

Preparation

Boil the pineapple juice in a saucepan over medium-high heat and then cook for 8 minutes until reduced to ⅓ cup. Remove it from the heat and then add garlic, cinnamon, allspice, oregano, thyme, oil, lime juice, and zest. Allow it to cool and mix ¼ cup of pineapple juice mixture with jerk sauce in a suitable bowl. Toss in the shrimp, mix well to coat, cover, and refrigerate for 30 minutes. Mix black beans with rice, salt, black pepper and remaining pineapple juice mixture in a suitable bowl. Set up a grill over medium heat and thread the shrimp, scallions, and pineapples over the skewers. Grill the shrimp skewers for 5 minutes per side. Set a bed of lettuce in a plate. Top this lettuce with rice bean salad. Top the salad with skewers and garnish with lime slices. Enjoy.

Soups

Jamaican Chicken and Pumpkin Soup

Preparation time: 10 minutes
Cook time: 35 minutes
Nutrition facts (per serving): 576 Cal (38g fat, 38g protein, 3g fiber)

If you haven't tried the classic Jamaican chicken and pumpkin soup before, then here comes a simple and easy to cook recipe that you can recreate at home in no time with minimum efforts.

Ingredients (6 servings)
3 pounds chicken thighs, cut in chunks
1 medium onion, diced
2 teaspoon garlic, minced
2 teaspoon thyme
1 Scotch bonnet pepper
1 teaspoon smoked paprika
1 bay leaf
5 cups broth
3 green onions, diced
1 teaspoon all spice
1 chayote, cut into chunks
1 plantain, cut into chunks
3 cups butter squash, cut into chunks
2 carrots, cut into chunks
3 tablespoon parsley
1 flavored packet cock soup
Salt and black pepper, to taste

Preparation

Sauté the onion, bay leaf, allspice, thyme, green onions, garlic, and pepper in a skillet for 3 minutes. Stir in the chicken, black pepper, and salt, then cook for 1 minute. Add water and veggies to the cover and cook for 30 minutes. Serve warm.

Jamaican Gungo Peas Soup

Preparation time: 10 minutes
Cook time: 1 hour 20 minutes
Nutrition facts (per serving): 350 Cal (17g fat, 37g protein, 1.2g fiber)

Gungo peas soup is another popular entrée known for its mixture of Gungo peas with potatoes, yam, and carrot.

Ingredients (6 servings)

3 cups Gungo peas

8 cups vegetable broth

1 cup coconut milk

1 medium onion, chopped

2 green onions, chopped

¼ cup red bell pepper, diced

2 garlic cloves, minced

1 potato, cut in cubes

1 cup yam, chopped

1 carrot, diced

1 teaspoon dried thyme

1 whole Scotch bonnet pepper

6 pimento berries

½ teaspoon fresh ginger, grated

6 flour dumplings

Sea salt, to taste

Preparation

Soak the Gungo peas in water in a large bowl overnight. Rinse and drain the peas and then transfer to a cooking pot. Add water to cover the gungo peas and cook for 1 hour. Stir in the rest of the ingredients and then cook to a boil. Reduce its heat and cook for 20 minutes. Serve warm.

Coconut-Pumpkin Soup

Preparation time: 15 minutes
Cook time: 1 hour
Nutrition facts (per serving): 243 Cal (21g fat, 3.5g protein, 1g fiber)

This coconut pumpkin soup is one of the Jamaican specialties, so everyone must try this interesting combination of a calabaza with carrot and peppers.

Ingredients (4 servings)

2 tablespoon butter
1 tablespoon olive oil
2 stalks celery, chopped
2 large shallots, chopped
2 scallions, chopped
2 large garlic cloves, minced
1 carrot, peeled and chopped
4 cups calabaza, chopped
4 cups chicken stock
3 sprigs fresh thyme
2 bay leaves
1 Scotch bonnet chile pepper, stemmed
⅛ teaspoon ground allspice
1 pinch salt and black pepper s
1 (13.5 oz.) can coconut milk
1 lime, juiced

Preparation

Sauté the celery, garlic, carrot, scallions, and shallots with oil and butter in a large pot for 5 minutes. Stir in allspice, chile pepper, bay leaves, thyme, stock, and calabaza. Next, then cook to a boil. Cover and reduce its heat to low, cook for 45 minutes. Adjust the seasoning with black pepper and salt. Puree the cooked soup until smooth. Stir in the milk and lime juice and then cook for 5 minutes. Serve warm.

Jamaican Tortilla Soup

Preparation time: 15 minutes
Cook time: 26 minutes
Nutrition facts (per serving): 370 Cal (17g fat, 5g protein, 3g fiber)

Enjoy a delicious, juicy, and savory mix of veggies cooked with coconut milk. Serve with tortilla strips on top. Pair with white rice or fried rice.

Ingredients (8 servings)

3 boneless chicken breast halves
8 cups water
8 teaspoon chicken bouillon granules
1 cup carrot, chopped
¼ teaspoon ground allspice
½ teaspoon fresh thyme, chopped
⅛ teaspoon ground cinnamon
1 tablespoon fresh ginger, chopped
1 tablespoon garlic, minced
1 cup tomato, chopped
1 cup coconut milk
1 teaspoon hot pepper sauce
1 cup mozzarella cheese, shredded
2 cups crispy tortilla strips
2 limes, cut into wedges

Preparation

Set a grill over medium heat. Grill the prepared chicken for 8 minutes per side. Cut the grilled chicken into chunks. Add the chicken, carrot, bouillon, water, garlic, ginger, cinnamon, thyme, and allspices to a saucepan. Cook the chicken to a boil, reduce its heat to a simmer, and cook for 10 minutes. Stir in the hot pepper sauce, coconut milk, and tomato. Cook the mixture until warm. Divide the soup into serving bowls. Garnish with tortilla strips, mozzarella cheese, and lime wedges. Enjoy.

Jamaican Spinach Soup

Preparation time: 10 minutes
Cook time: 20 minutes
Nutrition facts (per serving): 124 Cal (6g fat, 2.6g protein, 0.8g fiber)

Here comes the famous spinach soup that can be served with white rice or fried rice. Add a drizzle of olive oil on top before serving.

Ingredients (6 servings)

3 tablespoon olive oil
1 onion, chopped
2 stalks celery, chopped
4 garlic cloves, minced
2 tablespoon fresh ginger root, minced
1 tablespoon turbinado sugar
2 teaspoon sea salt
¼ teaspoon ground turmeric
¼ teaspoon ground allspice
¼ teaspoon ground nutmeg
2 potatoes, peeled and diced
4 cups zucchini, chopped
6 cups vegetable stock
1 pinch cayenne pepper
1 cup fresh spinach, chopped
½ red bell pepper, minced

Preparation

Sauté the onion with oil, sugar, ginger, garlic, and celery in a large pot for 5 minutes. Stir in the nutmeg, allspice, turmeric, salt, zucchini, potatoes, and stock. Cook to a boil, reduce its heat, and cook for 10 minutes on a simmer. Add the spinach and cayenne pepper and then remove from the heat. After 3 minutes, blend the soup with a hand blender. Garnish with the bell pepper and serve warm.

Chicken Soup with Dumplings

Preparation time: 15 minutes
Cook time: 60 minutes
Nutrition facts (per serving): 381 Cal (3 g fat, 25 g protein, 2.8g fiber)

Yes, you can make something as delicious as this soup by using some popular Jamaican ingredients like kabocha squash, bonnet pepper, and potatoes.

Ingredients (6 servings)

3 pounds chicken thighs

2 cups Kabocha squash cubed

1 onion, chopped

2 garlic cloves, sliced

1 Russet potato, peeled and quartered

1 turnip, quartered

2 chicken bouillon cubes

6 fresh thyme, springs

2 medium carrots, peeled and sliced

1 Scotch bonnet pepper

6 Allspice berries

8 cups water

Salt, to taste

Cilantro for garnish

Flour dumplings

1 cup all-purpose flour

Salt, to taste

Water, as needed

Preparation

Sear the chicken with oil in a skillet until golden brown. Stir in 8 cups water, and squash then cook to a boil. Cover, reduce its heat, and cook for 30 minutes. Stir in the Scotch bonnet, chicken bouillon, carrots, thyme, garlic, potato, and onion. Mix the flour with salt and water in a suitable bowl until it makes a smooth dough. Divide the prepared dough into dumplings and add the dumplings to the soup with the allspice berries. Cook this soup for 25 minutes. Remove the pepper and garnish with cilantro. Enjoy.

Jamaican Vegetable Soup

Preparation time: 15 minutes
Cook time: 25 minutes
Nutrition facts (per serving): 381 Cal (6g fat, 24g protein, 0.6g fiber)

The Jamaican vegetable soup has no parallel in taste. It has a mix of jerk seasoning with beans and veggies.

Ingredients (6 servings)
Jamaican Soup
1 tablespoon oil
1 small yellow onion, diced
1 rib celery, chopped
½ green pepper, chopped
½ red pepper, chopped
2 garlic cloves, chopped
¼ cup jerk seasoning
4 ½ cups water
1 small can of corn, drained
2 ½ tablespoon bouillon
1 can red kidney beans, drained
4 ½ potatoes, peeled and chopped
2 vegan sausages, cooked and sliced
¼ cup canned coconut milk
⅓ cup cilantro, chopped
2 tablespoon fresh lime juice

Jerk Seasoning

1 tablespoon granulated onion

1 tablespoon granulated garlic

1 tablespoon dried parsley

1 ½ tablespoon brown sugar

2 teaspoon cayenne pepper

2 teaspoon chili powder

2 teaspoon dried thyme

2 teaspoon salt

1 teaspoon allspice

1 teaspoon black pepper

½ teaspoon cinnamon

½ teaspoon nutmeg

½ teaspoon cumin

⅛ teaspoon cloves

Preparation

Sauté the onion with black pepper, salt, oil, peppers, and celery in an Instant Pot on Sauté mode for 5 minutes. Stir in the garlic, jerk seasoning, potatoes, corn, beans, bouillon, and water. Mix well and seal the lid. Cook the soup for 5 minutes under high pressure. Release the steam naturally for 10 minutes. Stir in the rest of the soup ingredients and mix well. Serve warm.

Chicken Foot Soup

Preparation time: 15 minutes
Cook time: 22 minutes
Nutrition facts (per serving): 248 Cal (8g fat, 22g protein, 1g fiber)

A perfect mix of the chicken foot with corn, yam, and turnips in a single soup is all that you need to expand your Jamaican menu. Simple and easy to make, this recipe is a must to try.

Ingredients (8 servings)
8 cups chicken stock
1 lb. of chicken foot
2 corn cobs
¾ lb. yellow yam, diced
2 turnips, sliced
1 Scotch bonnet pepper
2 small carrots, diced
Salt, to taste
2 stalk escallion
1 sprig thyme
1 cock soup flavor mix
1 ½ lb. pumpkin, diced
1 ½ lb. flour
1 medium Irish, diced

Preparation
Boil the chicken foot with turnips, soup mix, yam, Scotch bonnet, turnips, pumpkin, corn, and stock in a saucepan. Mix the flour with enough water

until it makes smooth dough. Then cover and leave the prepared dough aside. Peel and cut the yams into cubes. Add the yams to the soup and cook for 10 minutes. Divide the prepared dough into dumplings and add them to the soup. Cover and cook for 10 minutes. Stir in the salt, black pepper, thyme, and scallion. Reduce its heat and cook for 2 minutes. Serve warm.

Jamaican Pumpkin Soup

Preparation time: 10 minutes
Cook time: 47 minutes
Nutrition facts (per serving): 368 Cal (21g fat, 28g protein, 1g fiber)

Serve the warming bowl of pumpkin pureed soup and make your meal a little more nutritional. It has everything healthy in it, ranging from pumpkin to potato and carrot.

Ingredients (6 servings)

2 tablespoon coconut oil
1 cup onion, minced
3 garlic cloves, minced
¼ cup celery, chopped
2 green onions, chopped
1 tablespoon freshly parsley, chopped
¼ teaspoon dried
4 cups Jamaican Pumpkin, peeled and diced
1 cup potato, peeled and chopped
1 cup carrot, diced
4 cups vegetable broth
½ cup coconut milk
1 whole Scotch bonnet pepper
¼ teaspoon ground allspice
Salt, to taste

Preparation

Sauté the garlic and onion with oil in a cooking pan for 4 minutes. Stir in the carrots and celery and then sauté for 3 minutes. Stir in the allspice, black pepper, coconut milk, stock, potato, pumpkin, thyme, parsley, and green onion and then cook to a boil. Reduce its heat and cook for 30 minutes. Remove the bonnet pepper and thyme sprig from the soup. Allow the soup to cool and puree the soup with a hand blender. Add salt and garnish with spring onion and coconut milk. Serve warm.

Jerk Sweet Potato Soup

Preparation time: 5 minutes
Cook time: 25 minutes
Nutrition facts (per serving): 345 Cal (21g fat, 26g protein, 2g fiber)

This Jamaican sweet potato soup is a typical Jamaican entree, which is a staple on a healthy menu. It has this rich mix of sweet potatoes with garlic and jerk seasoning.

Ingredients (4 servings)

3 medium sweet potatoes, peeled and diced
1 tablespoon butter
1 onion, sliced
2 garlic cloves, crushed
1 red chili, sliced
2 teaspoon Jerk seasoning
4 cups vegetable stock

Preparation

Add the sweet potatoes and the rest of the ingredients to a cooking pot and cook for 25 minutes. Puree the soup and serve warm.

Chicken Soup

Preparation time: 10 minutes
Cook time: 40 minutes
Nutrition facts (per serving): 430 Cal (29g fat, 27g protein, 3g fiber)

Try this Jamaican chicken soup with your favorite herbs on top. Adding a dollop of cream or yogurt will make it even richer in taste.

Ingredients (8 servings)
5 cups pumpkin cubed
12 cups water
2 ½ lbs. chicken cut up
2 scallions, chopped
3 sprigs thyme
1 teaspoon pimento berries
1 small Scotch bonnet pepper
½ lb. yellow yam, diced
½ lb. sweet potato, diced
½ lb. Irish potato, diced
1 carrot, diced
2 corn on the cob
1 pack chicken noodle soup
6 small chicken cubes
½ tablespoon salt
1 tablespoon butter

Dumplings

2 cups flour

½ teaspoon salt

½ cup 3 tablespoon water

Preparation

Add 8 cups water to a deep soup pot and boil on high heat. Add the pumpkin and cook for 20 minutes. Puree the pumpkin and add the chicken, bonnet pepper, pimento berries, thyme, and scallions. Next, cook for 10 minutes. Stir in the carrots, yam, and corn. Cook until the yam is soft. Mix the flour with water and salt to make the dough and divide the prepared dough into dumplings. Add these dumplings to the soup, along with the butter, salt, broth cubes, and soup mix. Lastly, cook for 10 minutes. Serve warm.

Jamaican Carrot Soup

Preparation time: 10 minutes
Cook time: 55 minutes
Nutrition facts (per serving): 225 Cal (4g fat, 14g protein, 3g fiber)

Enjoy this Jamaican carrot soup with crispy bread and a fresh vegetable salad on the side. The warming bowl of this soup makes a great serving for all the special dinners.

Ingredients (6 servings)
Soup
5 tablespoon unsalted butter
2 pounds carrots, sliced
1 large onion, sliced
Salt and black pepper, to taste
4 large scallions, sliced
½ Scotch bonnet chile, seeded and sliced
1 teaspoon soy sauce
1 teaspoon thyme, chopped
½ teaspoon ginger, minced
¼ teaspoon ground cumin
⅛ teaspoon ground allspice
⅛ teaspoon nutmeg, grated
6 cups chicken stock
1 small red potato, peeled and sliced
1 bay leaf
1 tablespoon fresh lemon juice

Pear Relish

4 ripe pears, peeled, cored and diced

4 teaspoon lemon juice

¼ cup parsley, chopped

¼ teaspoon ground allspice

⅛ teaspoon nutmeg, grated

Plantain Chips

1 large ripe plantain

Vegetable oil, for frying

Salt, to taste

Preparation

Sauté the onion, carrots, black pepper, and salt with butter in a deep saucepan on low heat for 30 minutes. Stir in the nutmeg, allspice, cumin, ginger, thyme, soy sauce, scallions, and Scotch bonnet and then sauté for 4 minutes. Stir in the bay leaf, potato, and stock, cover, and cook for 25 minutes. Remove it from heat and leave for about 10 minutes. Remove the bay leaf and puree the cooked soup with a hand blender. Add the lime juice and mix well. Toss the pears with lemon juice, nutmeg, allspice, and parsley in a suitable bowl. Peel the plantains and then slice diagonally. Sauté the plantain slices with oil in a skillet until golden brown. Transfer the plantains to a plate and drizzle salt on top. Divide the cooked soup between the bowls and garnish it with the pears and the plantain chips. Serve warm.

Caribbean Fish Soup

Preparation time: 15 minutes
Cook time: 45 minutes
Nutrition facts (per serving): 401 Cal (20g fat, 36g protein, 4g fiber)

You cannot expect to have Jamaican cuisine and not try the traditional fish tea soup in it. This fish soup is full of shrimp, fish, and potatoes.

Ingredients (6 servings)

1 tablespoon olive oil
1 medium onion, diced
1 large carrot peeled and diced
2 stalks celery, diced
2 tablespoon fresh thyme, minced
2 garlic cloves, minced
1 Scotch bonnet pepper, minced
2 cups Yukon gold potatoes, quartered
8 cups chicken broth
1 lb. raw shrimp peeled, deveined
1 lb. raw mild white fish, cut in chunks
Salt and black pepper to taste
Cilantro, onion, and lime juice to serve

Preparation

Sauté the carrots, celery, and onion with oil, black pepper, and salt in a large soup pot for 9 minutes. Stir in thyme, garlic, and bonnet peppers and then sauté for 30 seconds. Add the potatoes and chicken broth and then cook to a boil. Stir in the shrimp, black pepper, and salt. Reduce its heat and cook for 30 minutes on low heat. Garnish with the lime juice, onion, and minced cilantro. Serve warm.

Curried Shrimp Mango Soup

Preparation time: 15 minutes
Cook time: 2 hours 20 minutes
Nutrition facts (per serving): 490 Cal (22g fat, 27g protein, 2g fiber)

Loaded with lots of calories, this curried shrimp mango soup makes an amazing serving for all your meals. Enjoy it warm with your favorite bread.

Ingredients (8 servings)
1 tablespoon olive oil
1 large onion, chopped
2 stalks celery, sliced
4 garlic cloves, chopped
1 serrano chile, minced
2 tablespoon curry powder
1 teaspoon dried thyme
2 cups seafood broth
1 (14-oz.) can lite coconut milk
3 ripe mangoes, diced
1 ¼ pounds raw shrimp, peeled and deveined
1 bunch scallions, sliced
¼ teaspoon salt

Preparation
Sauté the onion with celery and oil in a Dutch oven over medium heat for 5 minutes. Stir in the chiles, garlic, thyme, and curry powder. Next, sauté for 30 seconds. Stir in the mangoes, coconut milk, and broth and then cook on a simmer for 5 minutes. Puree 3 cups of this soup in a blender and return to

the soup. Stir in the shrimp and cook for 3 minutes. Garnish with salt and scallions. Serve warm.

Caribbean Beef Soup

Preparation time: 10 minutes
Cook time: 1 hour 20 minutes
Nutrition facts (per serving): 267 Cal (6g fat, 10g protein, 1.2g fiber)

Try this super tasty Jamaican beef soup prepared with beef and sweet potatoes and serve your family and to make your meals special. As a result, you'll never stop having it; that's how heavenly the combination tastes.

Ingredients (6 servings)

2 teaspoon oil

¾ cup onions, diced

6 sprigs thyme

2 pounds stew beef, cut up

½ cup yellow split peas

Salt, to taste

Black pepper to taste

6 cups water

1 lb. white sweet potatoes, peeled and cut into chunks

1 lb. plantains, peeled and cut into rounds

2 carrots, diced

8 okra, tops and tips removed

¼ cup green onions, sliced

Preparation

Sauté the onions with oil in a pressure cooker for 3 minutes. Stir in 3 sprigs of thyme and then sauté for 1 minute. Stir in the beef and then sauté for 3 minutes. Stir in the split peas, black pepper, salt, and 5 cups water, secure the lid, and then cook for 22 minutes. Once done, release the pressure naturally. Remove the lid and add the thyme, carrots, water, plantains, and sweet potatoes. Then cook for 15 minutes. Stir in the okra and cook for 8 minutes. Garnish with the green onions and serve warm.

Ham and Bean Soup

Preparation time: 15 minutes
Cook time: 20 minutes
Nutrition facts (per serving): 312 Cal (9g fat, 20g protein, 9g fiber)

You can give this ham and bean soup a try because it has a good and delicious combination of cod fillet and a savory sour sauce.

Ingredients (6 servings)

1 small onion, chopped
1 tablespoon canola oil
3 cups cooked ham, cubed
2 cans (16 oz.) refried beans
1 can (14 ½ oz.) chicken broth
1 can (11 oz.) Mexican, drained
1 can (7 oz.) white corn, drained
1 can (4 oz.) green chiles, chopped
½ cup salsa
1 teaspoon Caribbean jerk seasoning
1 can (2 ¼ oz.) ripe olives, drained, sliced
⅓ cup lime juice
Sour cream and lime slices

Preparation

Sauté the onion with oil in a Dutch oven for 4 minutes. Stir in the jerk seasoning, salsa, chiles, corn, broth, refried beans, and ham. Then cook to a boil. Reduce its heat and cook for 5 minutes with occasional stirring. Stir in the lime juice and olives and then cook until warm. Garnish with the lime slices and the sour cream. Serve warm.

Pepper Pot Soup

Preparation time: 15 minutes
Cook time: 32 minutes
Nutrition facts (per serving): 381 Cal (6g fat, 23g protein, 1g fiber)

If you're bored with the usual soup recipes, then this Jamaican pepper pot soup recipe is one unique option. Enjoy it with fried rice or noodles on the side.

Ingredients (4 servings)
2 tablespoon vegetable oil
6 scallions, chopped
3 sprigs thyme, stems removed
2 garlic cloves, minced
1 small white onion, chopped
8 oz. fresh callaloo, chopped
4 cups vegetable stock
3 Scotch bonnet chiles, minced
1 yellow yam, peeled and cut into cubes
Salt and black pepper, to taste

Preparation
Sauté the scallion, onion, and garlic with oil in a large saucepan for 7 minutes. Stir in the halved chile, stock, and callaloo. Bring this mixture to a simmer and cook for 10 minutes. Discard the chiles and puree the rest of the soup with a hand blender. Add the yam and cook for 15 minutes. Adjust the seasoning with black pepper and salt. Garnish with the minced chiles. Serve warm.

Caribbean Callaloo Soup

Preparation time: 15 minutes
Cook time: 40 minutes
Nutrition facts (per serving): 395 Cal (11g fat, 24g protein, 1g fiber)

The delicious callaloo soup fish will satisfy your crabmeat cravings in no time. It's quick to make at home.

Ingredients (4 servings)

½ lb. bacon, cut into small bits
1 medium onion, diced
1 red bell pepper, diced
2 ribs celery, diced
1 lb. okra, sliced ½-inch thick
1 tablespoon garlic, chopped
¼ cup all-purpose flour
2 quarts vegetable stock
1 tablespoon Jamaican Pickapeppa sauce
2 cans (14 oz.) unsweetened coconut milk
2 tablespoon fresh thyme, chopped
2 bay leaves
1 lb. crabmeat, picked over for shells
4 lbs. baby spinach
Salt and black pepper, to taste
2 tablespoon hot pepper sauce

Preparation

Sauté the bacon in a soup pot until brown and crispy. Stir in the onion and sauté for 5 minutes. Stir in the garlic, okra, celery, and pepper. Then sauté for 3 minutes. Stir in the flour and then mix well for 5 minutes. Add the stock, coconut milk, thyme, Pickapeppa sauce, and bay leaves, and then cook for 15 minutes on a simmer. Add the crabmeat and the spinach leaves and then cook for 2 minutes. Adjust the seasoning with black pepper, hot pepper sauce, and salt. Serve warm.

Red Pea Soup with Spinners

Preparation time: 5 minutes
Cook time: 1 hour 15 minutes
Nutrition facts (per serving): 206 Cal (15g fat, 21g protein, 1g fiber)

Try the Jamaican red pea soup and cook it quickly to serve at your dinner table. Serve this dish with sautéed asparagus and mushrooms.

Ingredients (4 servings)
2 cans of kidney beans, drained and rinsed
1 quart of chicken stock
2 medium onions, chopped
3 scallions, chopped
2 carrots, chopped
2 teaspoon dried thyme
1 Scotch bonnet pepper
Salt and black pepper to taste
½ lb. of potatoes
½ lb. of yams, diced
½ cup coconut milk

Dumplings
1 cup flour
Water, as required

Preparation
Add the kidney beans and chicken stock to a saucepan. Then cook for 15 minutes. Meanwhile, mix the flour, water, and a pinch of salt in a suitable

bowl until smooth. Divide the prepared dough into 2 inch and ⅛-inch pieces and add them to the soup. Stir in the veggies and cook on a simmer for 1 hour. Serve warm.

Jamaican Mutton Soup

Preparation time: 15 minutes
Cook time: 1 hour 25 minutes
Nutrition facts (per serving): 228 Cal (6g fat, 14g protein, 3g fiber)

Here's a famous Jamaican mutton soup recipe that's mostly served at the dinner table. It has a blend of rich and nutritious ingredients like yam, carrot, and mutton.

Ingredients (6 servings)

2 ½ lbs. mutton
7 cups water
2 tablespoon red meat seasoning

Soup

1 lb. yam, chopped
1 Chocho chopped
1 medium potato
2 medium carrot, chopped
3 scallions, chopped
1 small onion, chopped
8 sprigs of thyme tied in a bundle
8 pimento berries
5 cups water
5 cups mutton stock
3 tablespoon pumpkin soup mix
Scotch bonnet
Black pepper, garlic powder and pink salt to taste

Dumplings

2 cups gluten-free flour

½ cup water

½ teaspoon pink salt

Preparation

Add the water, seasoning, and mutton to the Instant Pot. Secure the lid and cook on Meat mode for 20 minutes. Once done, release the pressure completely. Skim the fat from the top. Empty the pot, add 5 cups mutton stock, 5 cups water to a cooking pot, and add the rest of the veggies, thyme, soup mix, and berries. Next, cook on medium-low heat. Mix the flour with a pinch and enough water to make smooth dough. Divide the prepared dough into small, flattened dumplings. Add the dumplings to the soup, along with mutton, and cook on a simmer for 1 hour. Adjust the seasoning with black pepper, garlic powder, and pink salt. Serve warm.

Main Dishes

Jamaican Oxtail Stew

Preparation time: 10 minutes
Cook time: 2 hours 36 minutes
Nutrition facts (per serving): 238 Cal (2g fat, 31g protein, 1g fiber)

If you haven't tried the oxtail stew before, then here comes a simple and easy cook recipe that you can recreate at home in no time with minimum effort.

Ingredients (6 servings)
3 pounds oxtails, cut into segments
Salt, to taste
Black pepper, to taste
3 tablespoon light brown sugar
2 Spanish onions, peeled and chopped
4 garlic cloves, peeled and minced
3 tablespoon fresh ginger, peeled and chopped
1 Scotch bonnet pepper, whole
3 sprigs fresh thyme
12 allspice berries
1 bunch scallions, trimmed and chopped
2 tablespoon white sugar
3 tablespoon soy sauce
1 tablespoon Worcestershire sauce
3 tablespoon flour
3 tablespoon tomato ketchup
10 ½ oz. can butter beans, rinsed and drained

Preparation

Mix the oxtails with black pepper and salt. Add the brown sugar to a Dutch oven and cook for 6 minutes until it darkens. Sir in 2 tablespoon boiling water and mix well. Then add the oxtails, mix well, and cook until the oxtail turns brown. Next, transfer to a bowl. Add the garlic, onions, ginger, thyme, allspice, and scallions to the Dutch oven and then sauté for 5 minutes. Add the oxtails and water then cover and cook for 1 hour on a simmer with occasional stirring. Stir in the Worcestershire sauce, soy sauce, and sugar and then cook for 1 hour. Mix the flour with 1 one cup cooking liquid in a small bowl and pour into the stew. Add ketchup, mix well, and cook for 15 minutes until it thickens. Lastly, stir in the butter beans and bonnet pepper. serve warm.

Caribbean Fish Stew

Preparation time: 15 minutes
Cook time: 10 minutes
Nutrition facts (per serving): 357 Cal (5g fat, 21g protein, 0g fiber)

This Caribbean fish stew is a healthy entrée that can be served with some tasty salad on the side, which will enhance its flavor and will make it more nutritious.

Ingredients (6 servings)

½ teaspoon black pepper

¼ teaspoon ground red pepper

½ teaspoon ground cumin

1 ½ teaspoon salt

¾ lb. Alaskan salmon fillet, cut into pieces

¾ lb. red snapper fillet, cut into pieces

3 tablespoon olive oil

1 medium onion, sliced

1 red bell pepper, cut into ¾-inch pieces

2 teaspoon fresh thyme leaves

2 garlic cloves, minced

1 jalapeño pepper, minced

1 (13.5-oz.) can coconut milk

1 (14.5-oz.) can petite diced tomatoes, undrained

¼ cup cilantro leaves, chopped

1 tablespoon lime juice

Fresh cilantro, Garnish

Preparation

Mix the salt, cumin, red pepper, and black pepper in a suitable bowl. Rub this mixture over the fish and sear it in a skillet with 1 ½ tablespoon oil for 2 minutes per side. Sauté the onion with 1 ½ tablespoon in a Dutch oven until soft. Stir in the jalapeno, pepper, garlic, and thyme. Then sauté for 1 minute. Add the tomatoes, salt, coconut milk, and fish. Cover and cook for 3 minutes. Garnish with cilantro and lime juice. Serve warm.

Squash Coconut Stew

Preparation time: 15 minutes
Cook time: 55 minutes
Nutrition facts (per serving): 379 Cal (11g fat, 26g protein, 6g fiber)

This squash coconut stew is known as a classic Jamaican entrée. The pineapple slices with brown rice and coconut cream make a great serving for the table.

Ingredients (4 servings)
1 can of pineapple slices
1 Knorr vegetable stock cube
4 ½ oz. brown rice
5 ½ oz. butternut squash cubes
1 oz. solid coconut cream
1 Romano pepper
1 red Chili, minced
1 tomato, diced
½ tablespoon curry powder
⅓ oz. coriander
2 teaspoon ground coriander
1 garlic clove
1 tomato paste sachet
1 tomato paste sachet

Preparation
Add the rinsed brown rice and water to a saucepan and then cook to a boil. Reduce its heat and cook for 25 minutes. Drain and keep the rice aside.

Remove the seeds from the Romano peppers and cut them into pieces. Sauté the peppers and the squash with the oil in a pan for 5 minutes. Add the rest of the ingredients and cook until the squash gets tender. Serve warm.

Jamaican Jerk Chicken

Preparation time: 10 minutes
Cook time: 40 minutes
Nutrition facts (per serving): 303 Cal (7g fat, 33g protein, 1g fiber)

Here's a delicious chicken meal loaded with calories. Serve the chicken with hot bread for the best experience.

Ingredients (8 servings)
1 medium onion, chopped
3 medium scallions, chopped
2 Scotch bonnet chiles, chopped
2 garlic cloves, chopped
1 tablespoon five-spice powder
1 tablespoon allspice berries, ground
1 tablespoon ground pepper
1 teaspoon dried thyme, crumbled
1 teaspoon grated nutmeg
1 teaspoon salt
½ cup soy sauce
1 tablespoon vegetable oil
Two 4-lbs. chickens, quartered

Preparation
Blend the onions, scallions, allspice, thyme, nutmeg, salt, pepper, five-spice powder, garlic, and chiles in a blender. Stir in the soy sauce and pour this marinade into a shallow dish. Add the chicken, mix well, cover, and refrigerate overnight. Set up a grill on medium heat and grease its grates.

Grill the chicken for 40 minutes and flip once cooked halfway through. Serve warm.

Jamaican Smothered Oxtail

Preparation time: 15 minutes
Cook time: 8 hours 17 minutes
Nutrition facts (per serving): 859 Cal (21g fat, 96g protein, 3g fiber)

Have you tried the basic Jamaican smothered oxtail? Well, here's a Jamaican delight that adds oxtail with sauces to your dinner table in a delicious way.

Ingredients (4 servings)
2 ½ pounds beef oxtails
1 ¼ cups all-purpose flour
2 tablespoon Worcestershire sauce
2 teaspoon salt
1 teaspoon black pepper
¾ cup vegetable oil
3 cups beef broth
1 large onion, sliced
3 garlic cloves, minced

Preparation
Season the oxtail with 1 teaspoon black pepper, 2 teaspoon salt, and Worcestershire sauce. Drizzle ¼ cup flour over the oxtail. Sauté and sear the oxtail in a deep pan with oil until golden brown and then transfer it to a slow cooker. Sauté the onion and the garlic in the same pan and sauté until soft. Add the remaining flour to the pan and mix well. Stir in the broth and mix until lump-free. Pour this mixture over the oxtail in the slow cooker and cook for 8 hours on high. Serve warm.

Jamaican Hot Pepper Shrimp

Preparation time: 10 minutes
Cook time: 12 minutes
Nutrition facts (per serving): 491 Cal (33g fat, 29g protein, 2g fiber)

This hot pepper shrimp meal is known as the classic Jamaican dinner. Enjoy the shrimp with cucumber salad or roasted asparagus on the side.

Ingredients (2 servings)

1 lb. of raw shrimp, peeled and deveined
3 red Scotch bonnets chopped
½ tablespoon onion powder
½ tablespoon garlic granules or powder
2 teaspoon Himalayan pink salt
½ teaspoon black pepper
1 tablespoon sweet paprika
3 garlic cloves, minced
¼ teaspoon of allspice
½ tablespoon of thyme
1 teaspoon of old bay seasoning
¼ cup of warm water
2 tablespoon of coconut oil

Preparation

Mix the shrimp with the rest of the seasoning in a suitable bowl to coat well. Sauté the shrimp with 2 tablespoon coconut oil in a Dutch oven for 2 minutes. Stir in ¼ cup warm water, cover, and cook for 10 minutes on low heat. Serve warm.

Jamaican-Style Chickpea Curry

Preparation time: 15 minutes
Cook time: 26 minutes
Nutrition facts (per serving): 360 Cal (21g fat, 21g protein, 1g fiber)

If you haven't tried the famous chickpea curry before, then here comes a simple and easy cook recipe that you can recreate at home in no time with minimum effort.

Ingredients (4 servings)

2 tablespoon coconut oil
½ medium onion, chopped
3 garlic cloves, minced
1 teaspoon ginger, grated
2 spring onions, chopped
2 tablespoon curry powder
1 teaspoon ground paprika
2 sprigs of fresh thyme
1 medium tomato, chopped
1 medium carrot, diced
2 15-oz. cans chickpeas
1 14 oz. can coconut milk
½ cup water
6 allspice berries
¼ teaspoon Cayenne pepper
¾ teaspoon salt

Preparation

Sauté the onions with the oil in a large pot for 3 minutes. Add the spring onion, ginger, and garlic and then cook for 1 minute. Add the thyme, paprika, and curry powder and then cook for 2 minutes. Stir in the chickpeas, carrot, tomatoes, water, allspice berries, and coconut milk before cooking to a boil. Reduce its heat and cook for 15 minutes on a simmer with occasional stirring. Adjust the seasoning with black pepper and salt. Serve warm.

Jamaican Rice and Beans

Preparation time: 15 minutes
Cook time: 2 hours 26 minutes
Nutrition facts (per serving): 275 Cal (23g fat, 15g protein, 1g fiber)

The Jamaican rice and beans sound delicious to serve at the dinner table. It's known for its comforting taste and the energizing combination of ingredients.

Ingredients (4 servings)
8 oz. small dried red beans
1-quart water
16 oz. chicken stock
½ cup coconut cream
2 teaspoon fresh thyme leaves
½ teaspoon ground allspice
2 scallions, chopped
½ cup white onion, chopped
2 minced garlic cloves
1 teaspoon black pepper
1 ½ teaspoon salt
1 Scotch bonnet pepper
1 teaspoon brown sugar
Two ¼ cups uncooked long grain rice

Preparation
Rinse the beans and transfer them to a stockpot. Pour enough water to cover and cook for 3 minutes. Rinse and sort the beans and place them in a

stockpot. Add water to half fill the pot, cover, and cook for 3 minutes. Then remove from the heat and leave for 1 hour. Drain and rinse the cooked beans. Boil the coconut cream with the water and the chicken stock in a cooking pot. Stir in the beans, cover, and cook on medium heat for 2 hours. Stir in the rice, black pepper, salt, brown sugar, Scotch bonnet, garlic, onion, scallion, allspice, and thyme. Add more water, if needed, to keep the rice submerged. Cook to a boil, reduce its heat and cover to cook for 20 minutes. Serve warm.

Jamaican Curry Chick

Preparation time: 10 minutes
Cook time: 36 minutes
Nutrition facts (per serving): 388 Cal (11g fat, 28g protein, 3g fiber)

This Jamaican curry chicken is everything you must be looking for to make your dinner loaded with nutrients. The combination of chicken with coconut milk and potatoes make a complete package for a health enthusiast like me.

Ingredients (4 servings)

1 ¼ pounds boneless chicken breasts, cut into pieces

1 teaspoon salt

2 tablespoon olive oil

1 yellow onion, chopped

1 red bell pepper, chopped

2 jalapeno peppers, chopped

3 garlic cloves, minced

1 teaspoon fresh ginger, minced

3 ½ tablespoon curry powder

1 teaspoon turmeric

¾ teaspoon allspice

¼ teaspoon cayenne pepper

2 medium Yukon gold potatoes, peeled and diced

1 15-oz. can light coconut milk

1 tablespoon Worcestershire sauce

1 ½ teaspoon white wine vinegar

1 teaspoon hot sauce

ped fresh cilantro

eparation

Season the chicken with salt. Sauté the onion with the oil in a Dutch oven for 5 minutes. Stir in the ginger, garlic, jalapenos, and bell pepper. Then sauté for 2 minutes. Add the cayenne, allspice, turmeric, and curry powder. Sauté for 1 minute. Add the chicken and then sauté for 5 minutes. Stir in the potatoes and then sauté for 3 minutes. Add the hot sauce, vinegar, Worcestershire sauce, and coconut milk. Mix well and cook for 20 minutes. Garnish with cilantro.

Jerk Chicken Wings

Preparation time: 15 minutes
Cook time: 55 minutes
Nutrition facts (per serving): 405 Cal (4g fat, 23g protein, 2g fiber)

These chicken drumettes are loved by all, young and adult. They're simple and quick to make. This delight is great to serve at dinner tables.

Ingredients (6 servings)

½ yellow onion, chopped
½ cup green onions, sliced
6 garlic cloves
3 habanero peppers, seeded and chopped
2 tablespoon fresh thyme leaves
1 tablespoon salt
2 teaspoon ground black pepper
2 teaspoon ground allspice
1 teaspoon dried thyme
½ teaspoon ground cinnamon
½ teaspoon ground cumin
½ teaspoon grated nutmeg
2 tablespoon vegetable oil
3 tablespoon soy sauce
2 tablespoon brown sugar
⅓ cup lime juice
3 pounds chicken wing drumettes
Cooking spray

Preparation

Blend the yellow onion with the lime juice, brown sugar, soy sauce, vegetable oil, nutmeg, cumin, cinnamon, dried thyme, allspice, black pepper, salt, thyme, habanero peppers, garlic, and green onions in a blender until smooth. Add the chicken, mix well, cover, and refrigerate for 8 hours. At 450 degrees F, preheat your oven. Layer a baking sheet with aluminum foil and grease with cooking spray. Place the marinated chicken in the baking sheet, reserve its marinade, and bake the chicken for 25 minutes. Brush ½ of the reserved marinade over the chicken, flip, and bake for 15 minutes. Brush the other half of the marinade over the chicken, flip, and bake for 15 minutes. Serve warm.

Spicy Shrimp Skewers

Preparation time: 15 minutes
Cook time: 10 minutes
Nutrition facts (per serving): 389 Cal (13g fat, 23g protein, 2g fiber)

If you haven't tried the famous spicy shrimp skewers before, then here comes a simple and easy to cook recipe that you can recreate at home in no time with minimum efforts.

Ingredients (4 servings)
⅓ cup lime juice
⅓ cup honey
1 teaspoon soy sauce
1 teaspoon vegetable oil
2 tablespoon Jamaican jerk seasoning
3 dashes hot pepper sauce
Salt and black pepper to taste
2 pounds large shrimp, peeled and deveined

Preparation
Mix the soy sauce with oil, honey, and lime juice in a suitable bowl. Stir in the salt, black pepper, hot pepper sauce, and jerk seasoning. Toss in the shrimp and then mix well to coat. Cover and refrigerate the shrimp for 1 hour. Thread the marinated shrimp on the wooden skewers. Set up a grill over medium-high heat. Grill the shrimp skewers for 5 minutes per side. Serve warm.

Jamaican Fried Snapper

Preparation time: 15 minutes
Cook time: 17 minutes
Nutrition facts (per serving): 310 Cal (6g fat, 32g protein, 0g fiber)

It's basically a spicy fried snapper meal, and it's known for its super-nutritious blend of ingredients. It tastes great when served with a dollop of cream or yogurt.

Ingredients (4 servings)

1 (1 ½ pound) whole red snapper, cleaned and scaled
Salt and black pepper, to taste
1 quart vegetable oil for frying
1 teaspoon vegetable oil
½ white onion, sliced
⅛ teaspoon garlic, minced
½ large carrot, peeled and julienned
1 sprig fresh thyme, leaves stripped
1 allspice berry, cracked
¼ habanero pepper, seeded and minced
¼ cup white vinegar
1 tablespoon water
¾ teaspoon salt
1 pinch brown sugar

Preparation

Make 3 small slits on both sides of the fish and liberally rub it with black pepper and salt. Add 1-quart oil to a deep skillet over medium-high heat and cook the fish for 5 minutes per side. Remove the fish from the skillet and transfer it to a plate. Saute the garlic, carrot, and onion with 1 teaspoon oil in a large skillet for 2 minutes. Stir in the sugar, salt, water, vinegar, habanero pepper, allspice, and thyme. Finally, cook for 5 minutes. Add the onion mixture on top of the fish. Serve.

Jamaican Oxtail Fry

Preparation time: 15 minutes
Cook time: 40 minutes
Nutrition facts (per serving): 361 Cal (22g fat, 34 protein, 2g fiber)

This oxtail is a must to have on this Jamaican menu. It has a delicious mix of oxtail with spices and ginger root.

Ingredients (4 servings)

1 lb. beef oxtail, cut into pieces
1 large onion, chopped
1 green onion, sliced
2 garlic cloves, minced
1 teaspoon ginger root, minced
1 Scotch bonnet chile pepper, chopped
2 tablespoon soy sauce
1 sprig fresh thyme, chopped
½ teaspoon salt
1 teaspoon black pepper
2 tablespoon vegetable oil
1 cups water
1 teaspoon whole allspice berries
1 tablespoon cornstarch
2 tablespoon water

Preparation

Sauté the onion, oxtails, black pepper, salt, thyme, soy sauce, chile pepper, ginger, garlic, and green onion with the oil in a pressure cooker for 10 minutes. Add the water, seal the lid, and then cook for 25 minutes. Once done, release the pressure and remove the lid. Add the allspice berries and then cook on medium-high heat. Mix the cornstarch with 2 tablespoon water in a suitable bowl. Pour into the cooker and cook for 5 minutes until it thickens. Serve warm.

Grilled Pork Loin Chops

Preparation time: 15 minutes
Cook time: 10 minutes
Nutrition facts (per serving): 493 Cal (15g fat, 30g protein, 1.7g fiber)

A perfect mix of pork loin chops with jerk seasoning is a must to try. Serve warm with your favorite side salad for the best taste.

Ingredients (4 servings)

½ (12 oz.) bottle lager beer
3 fluid oz. dark rum
¼ cup molasses
¼ cup soy sauce
¼ cup lime juice
2 tablespoon garlic, minced
2 tablespoon ginger, minced
1 Scotch bonnet chile pepper, minced
2 teaspoon fresh thyme, chopped
2 teaspoon fresh marjoram, chopped
1½ teaspoon ground allspice
2 teaspoon ground cinnamon
1 teaspoon ground nutmeg
2 bay leaves
8 (6 oz.) pork loin chops
Salt and black pepper, to taste

Preparation

Add the lime juice, soy sauce, molasses, rum, and beer in a suitable bowl. Stir in the marjoram, thyme, scotch bonnet pepper, ginger, garlic, bay leaves, nutmeg, cinnamon, and allspice. Mix well and add to a Ziploc bag. Add the pork chops to the bag, seal, and refrigerate overnight. Set up a grill over medium heat. Remove the chops from the marinade and rub them with black pepper and salt. Grill the chops for 5 minutes per side. Serve warm.

Jamaican Goat Curry

Preparation time: 15 minutes
Cook time: 2 hours 15 minutes
Nutrition facts (per serving): 357 Cal (10g fat, 33g protein, 2g fiber)

The Jamaican goat curry is famous for its unique taste and aroma, and now you can bring those exotic flavors home by using this recipe.

Ingredients (6 servings)

3 pounds bone-in goat meat, cubed
½ cup white vinegar
1 large onion, chopped
½ cup Jamaican curry powder
2 Scotch bonnet peppers, seeded and chopped
3 garlic cloves, chopped
6 allspice berries
½ teaspoon salt
½ teaspoon black pepper, to taste
4 sprigs fresh thyme, leaves stripped
2 tablespoon vegetable oil
2 large potatoes, diced
2 carrots, diced
Water, to cover

Preparation

Mix the goat meat with vinegar in a large bowl and pour water to cover the meat. Leave for 5 minutes and then drain. Mix the onion with thyme, black pepper, salt, allspice berries, garlic, bonnet peppers, and 6 tablespoon curry powder in a suitable bowl. Rub this mixture over the goat meat. Cover and refrigerate the meat for 8 hours. Sauté 2 tablespoon curry powder with oil in a skillet for 1 minute. Stir in the goat meat and then cook for 2 minutes per side. Add the remaining spice rub, carrots, and potatoes. Pour enough water to cover the meat and cook to a boil. Reduce its heat, cover and cook for 2 hours. Serve warm.

Jamaican Apple Rice

Preparation time: 10 minutes
Cook time: 30 minutes
Nutrition facts (per serving): 428 Cal (18g fat, 26g protein, 1g fiber)

Have you tried apple rice before? Well, now you can enjoy this unique and flavorsome combination by cooking this recipe at home.

Ingredients (2 servings)
1 tablespoon vegetable oil
½ large onion, sliced
½ red apple, cored and sliced
1 pinch curry powder
1 cup water
⅔ cup brown rice
1 teaspoon dark molasses
1 small banana, sliced
1 tablespoon unsweetened flaked coconut

Preparation
Sauté the onion and the red apple with oil in a saucepan over medium heat until soft. Stir in the water, curry powder, rice, and molasses. Then cover and cook for 30 minutes until liquid is absorbed. Add banana and coconut on top. Serve.

Jamaican Coconut Rice

Preparation time: 15 minutes

Cook time: 20 minutes

Nutrition facts (per serving): 352 Cal (24g fat, 31g protein, 0.6g fiber)

The coconut rice is so delicious and perfect to complete your menu; and this one, in particular, is great to have on a nutritious diet. It's best to serve a large number of guests.

Ingredients (4 servings)

1 ½ cups long grain rice

2 cups fresh coconut milk

1 teaspoon salt

1 tablespoon coconut oil

1 stalk scallion, chopped

Preparation

Boil the coconut milk with salt and coconut oil in a deep pan. Rinse and add the rice to the milk. Then cover to cook on medium heat until the liquid is absorbed. Garnish with scallion and serve warm.

Jamaican Jerk Shrimp in Foil

Preparation time: 15 minutes
Cook time: 13 minutes
Nutrition facts (per serving): 299 Cal (16g fat, 24g protein, 3g fiber)

Now you can quickly make flavorsome jerk shrimp at home and serve it to have a fancy meal for yourself and your guest.

Ingredients (4 servings)

1 cup soy sauce
¾ cup distilled vinegar
1 medium white onion, chopped
¼ cup olive oil
4 green onions, chopped
2 tablespoon dried thyme
2 habanero peppers, stemmed
1 tablespoon brown sugar
1 tablespoon ground nutmeg
1 teaspoon ground allspice
1 teaspoon ground cloves
1 lb. uncooked medium shrimp, peeled and deveined
Heavy-duty aluminum foil

Preparation

On medium-high heat, preheat a grill. Mix the soy sauce, cloves, allspice, nutmeg, sugar, habanero peppers, thyme, green onions, olive oil, onion, and vinegar in a food processor for 15 seconds. Make a bowl using a foil tin and add shrimp to this bowl. Drizzle half of the jerk seasoning over the shrimp.

Pack the shrimp in the foil, place it in the grill, and cook for 10 minutes. Cook the remaining seasoning mixture in a saucepan and cook for 3 minutes, and then pour over the grilled shrimp. Serve warm.

Curried Goat

Preparation time: 10 minutes
Cook time: 1 hour 35 minutes
Nutrition facts (per serving): 326 Cal (17g fat, 23g protein, 2g fiber)

This curried goat meal will melt your heart away with its epic flavors. The goat meat is cooked with jerk seasoning and lots of veggies to make it taste even better and nutritious.

Ingredients (6 servings)
Jerk Seasoning
1 medium onion, chopped

2 tablespoon garlic, chopped

1 tablespoon ginger, chopped

10 sprigs thyme, leaves stripped

1 Scotch bonnet pepper, stemmed

1 tablespoon black pepper

1 tablespoon brown sugar

1 teaspoon salt

1 teaspoon ground allspice

½ teaspoon cayenne pepper

Curried Goat
5 pounds goat leg, cut into cubes

5 tablespoon Caribbean curry powder

1 cup vegetable oil

1 cup carrot, diced

3 cups yellow onion, diced

4 cups russet potato, diced

1 cup scallion, chopped

Preparation

Blend the onions with the jerk seasoning ingredients in a food processor. Mix the goat meat with jerk seasoning and 3 tablespoon curry powder in a large bowl. Cover and refrigerate the meat for 4 hours. Sauté 2 tablespoon curry powder in a stockpot. Stir in the goat meat and 2 cups water and then cook to a simmer. Cover and cook for 1 hour. Add the potato, onion, and carrot and then cook for 30 minutes. Stir in the scallion and then cook for 5 minutes. Serve warm.

Jerk Chicken Thighs with Tropical Chutney

Preparation time: 15 minutes
Cook time: 48 minutes
Nutrition facts (per serving): 293 Cal (13g fat, 14g protein, 7g fiber)

If you haven't tried the jerk chicken thighs with tropical chutney, then here comes a simple and easy to cook recipe that you can recreate at home in no time with minimum efforts.

Ingredients (6 servings)
Jerk Chicken
2 tablespoon ground allspice
2 tablespoon brown sugar
2 tablespoon garlic powder
1 tablespoon onion powder
1 tablespoon salt
1 teaspoon ground cumin
½ teaspoon ground ginger
½ teaspoon ground nutmeg
½ teaspoon black pepper
¼ teaspoon cayenne
¼ teaspoon ground cinnamon
¼ teaspoon ground cloves
1 cup orange juice
4 tablespoon olive oil
3 pounds boneless chicken thighs

Tropical Chutney

¼ cup red wine vinegar

¼ cup honey

¼ teaspoon ground coriander

¼ teaspoon ground cinnamon

¼ teaspoon ground cloves

1 cup mango, diced

1 cup papaya, diced

1 cup pineapple, diced

2 garlic cloves, chopped

1 jalapeno, diced

1 teaspoon fresh ginger, chopped

Salt and black pepper, to taste

Preparation

Blend the orange juice, 2 tablespoon olive oil, cloves, cinnamon, cayenne, black pepper, nutmeg, ginger, cumin, salt, onion powder, garlic powder, brown sugar, and allspice in a bag. Add the chicken to the bag, seal, and shake well. Marinate for 45 minutes. Sear the chicken with the remaining oil in a skillet for 4 minutes per side.

For the chutney, mix all its ingredients in a saucepan and cook for 40 minutes on low heat. Mash the mango mixture a little and then serve the chicken with mango chutney.

Jerk Turkey Legs

Preparation time: 15 minutes
Cook time: 50 minutes
Nutrition facts (per serving): 319 Cal (14g fat, 18g protein, 7g fiber)

Jamaican turkey legs are one good option to go for. Plus, if you have turkey legs and some basic spices at home, then you can make them in no time.

Ingredients (6 servings)

¼ cup vegetable oil
1 ½ tablespoon fresh thyme leaves
1 tablespoon light brown sugar
¾ teaspoon ground allspice
Juice of 3 limes
3 garlic cloves
2 Scotch bonnet peppers, stemmed
1 (1-inch) piece peeled ginger
1 bunch scallions, chopped
Salt and black pepper, to taste
6 turkey drumsticks (4 ½ pounds)
¼ cup fresh cilantro, chopped

Preparation

Blend the black pepper, salt, scallions, ginger, chile peppers, garlic, lime juice, allspice, brown sugar, thyme, and oil in a food processor until smooth. Rub this mixture over the turkey legs, cover, and refrigerate for 4 hours. At 425 degrees F, preheat your oven. Place the turkey legs on a greased baking sheet and then bake for 50 minutes. Garnish with lime wedges and cilantro.

Callaloo Chicken Roulade

Preparation time: 10 minutes
Cook time: 47 minutes
Nutrition facts (per serving): 402 Cal (21g fat, 12g protein, 5g fiber)

The callaloo chicken roulades are enjoyed with mixed roasted veggies, and they taste great. Have them at your dinner table for a tempting serving.

Ingredients (6 servings)

2 boneless skinless chicken breasts
Salt and black pepper, to taste
1 teaspoon adobo seasoning
½ teaspoon ground allspice
1 teaspoon dried basil
1 teaspoon dried oregano
¼ cup olive oil
1 small yellow onion, diced
3 garlic cloves, minced
3 cups callaloo, chopped (amaranth)
1 plum tomato, small diced
5 sprigs thyme
1 Scotch bonnet chile, seeded and julienned
2 tablespoon unsalted butter

Preparation

At 450 degrees f, preheat your oven. Place the chicken breasts in between plastic sheets and pound them with a mallet. Rub the chicken with oregano, salt, black pepper, allspice, adobo, and basil then place in a plate. Cover and refrigerate the chicken for 1 hour. Sauté the onions and the garlic with 2 tablespoon Oil in a Dutch oven for 5 minutes. Stir in the callaloo and mix well. Add the tomatoes, chiles, ½ cup water, and 2 sprigs thyme. Cook for 5 minutes, add the black pepper and salt, and then mix well. Spread this mixture on a baking sheet lined with parchment paper and then allow it to cool for 15 minutes. Place the flatten chicken on the working surface, top them with callaloo mixture, and roll the chicken. Seal the roll with a toothpick. Wrap each roulade with plastic sheet. To cook the roulade, boil the water in a saucepan and place the roulades in the water. Cook for 5 minutes and then remove the plastic. Sear the roulades in a skillet with 2 tablespoon oil for 10 minutes. Add the butter and the thyme. Then cook for 2 minutes. Bake the roulades for 10 minutes and then serve warm.

Escovitch Fish Sliders

Preparation time: 5 minutes
Cook time: 15 minutes
Nutrition facts (per serving): 376 Cal (14g fat, 22g protein, 18g fiber)

This fish slider recipe will make your day with its delightful taste. Serve warm with your favorite salad and chili sauce.

Ingredients (6 servings)
5 allspice berries
2 sprigs of fresh thyme
1 small Scotch bonnet chile, scored
2 garlic cloves (1 grated and 1 crushed)
1 tablespoon grated ginger
1 teaspoon sugar
½ cup malt vinegar
Salt and black pepper, to taste
1 carrot, cut into matchsticks
1 small red onion, sliced
1 small red bell pepper, sliced
1 small yellow bell pepper, sliced
¼ cup mayonnaise
1 tablespoon sweet chile sauce
Juice of ½ lime
1 scallion, minced
1 ¼ pounds thick snapper fillets
Vegetable oil, for brushing
One 12-oz. package (12 rolls) sweet dinner rolls

Preparation

Mix ¼ cup water, 1 teaspoon salt, vinegar, sugar, ginger, garlic, bonnet, thyme, and allspice in a small saucepan. Cook on a simmer for 2 minutes. Remove it from the heat and toss in the pepper, red onions, and carrots. Then mix well. Cover and refrigerate. Mix the mayonnaise with the scallions, lime juice, and chile sauce in a suitable bowl. Set up a grill over medium-high heat. Rub the snapper with crushed garlic, salt, black pepper, and oil. Grill the fish for 2 minutes per side. Cut the fish into pieces. Spread the prepared mayo mixture on the rolls and top it with the thyme and the relish. Add the fish and the pickled vegetables. Serve.

Jamaican Jerk Pit Chicken

Preparation time: 15 minutes
Cook time: 5 hours
Nutrition facts (per serving): 477 Cal (24g fat, 30g protein, 3g fiber)

If you want some new and exotic flavors in your meals, then this jerk pit chicken recipe is best to bring that variety to the menu.

Ingredients (6 servings)
Jamaican Jerk Paste
10 habanero chile peppers, pureed
6 tablespoon mustard seeds
4 tablespoon dried rosemary
4 tablespoon parsley, chopped
4 tablespoon dried basil
4 tablespoon dried thyme
6 scallions, chopped
2 teaspoon salt
2 teaspoon ground black pepper
½ cup yellow mustard
6 tablespoon orange juice
2 tablespoon lime juice
2 tablespoon cider vinegar

Chicken
2 cans beer
2 (3 ½ pounds) whole chickens

Preparation

Blend all the jerk paste in a blender and leave for 24 hours. Set up a charcoal grill over medium heat. Place the beer cans in the grill, set the chicken over these cans, and then cover. Grill the chicken for 4-5 hours until its internal temperature reaches 225 degrees F. Flip the chicken once cooked halfway through.

Grilled Beef with Jamaican Rum Glaze

Preparation time: 10 minutes
Cook time: 20 minutes
Nutrition facts (per serving): 492 Cal (39g fat, 32g protein, 1.2g fiber)

Here's another classic Jamaican beef filet recipe for your dinner and lunch. Serve it with a delicious salad and enjoy the best of it.

Ingredients (4 servings)

2 shallots minced
3 garlic cloves, minced
1 cup Myer's dark rum
3 cups chicken stock
2 tablespoon ancho puree
2 tablespoon molasses
Salt and black pepper, to taste
4 (8 oz.) filet mignon steaks

Preparation

Rub the steaks with black pepper and salt. Set up a grill over medium heat. Grill the steaks for 5 minutes per side. Sauté the garlic and the shallots with butter in a saucepan for 3 minutes. Stir in the rum and cook until reduced to ⅓ cup. Stir in the stock, cook to a boil, reduce its heat, and whisk in the remaining ingredients. Serve the steaks with sauce on top.

Jamaican Escovitch Fish with Pickled Vegetables

Preparation time: 15 minutes
Cook time: 13 minutes
Nutrition facts (per serving): 392 Cal (18g fat, 29g protein, 1g fiber)

Are you in a mood to have fish on the menu? Well, you can try this fish topped with veggies for a change and see how tasty it is.

Ingredients (4 servings)

1 ½ cups malt vinegar

2 teaspoon garlic powder

2 tablespoon 2 teaspoon sugar

2 teaspoon onion powder

1 teaspoon ground dried oregano

2 tablespoon 1 teaspoon salt

1 tablespoon pickling spice

1 teaspoon ground white pepper

1 red bell pepper, sliced

¼ cup vegetable oil, or more as needed

1 yellow bell pepper, sliced

1 green bell pepper, sliced

1 yellow onion, sliced

2 garlic cloves, sliced

1 Scotch bonnet pepper, pierced

6 (6-oz.) firm white fish fillets

1 lime, juiced

Freshly ground white pepper, to taste

1 cup all-purpose flour

1 tablespoon Emeril's® Original Essence

Creole Seasoning

2 ½ tablespoon paprika

2 tablespoon salt

2 tablespoon garlic powder

1 tablespoon black pepper

1 tablespoon onion powder

1 tablespoon cayenne pepper

1 tablespoon dried oregano

1 tablespoon dried thyme

Preparation

Mix the sugar, vinegar, 1 tablespoon 2 teaspoon salt, bell peppers, onion, pickling spice, garlic, and Scotch bonnet. Next, cook to a boil. Reduce its heat, cook for 2 minutes, and then remove from the heat. Place the fish in a baking dish and rub it with the white pepper. Mix the flour with the remaining spices in a suitable bowl. Coat the fish with this flour mixture and shake off the excess. Sear the fish in a skillet with oil for 3 minutes per side. Serve the fish with vegetables.

Vegetable Run-Up

Preparation time: 10 minutes
Cook time: 70 minutes
Nutrition facts (per serving): 344 Cal (41g fat, 34g protein, 3g fiber)

Try the Jamaican vegetable mix and cook it quickly to serve at your dinner table. Serve this meal with sautéed asparagus and mushrooms.

Ingredients (4 servings)

4 cups coconut milk

1 tablespoon whole allspice berries

4 scallions, chopped

3 sprigs thyme

2 garlic cloves, minced

2 plum tomatoes, peeled, seeded, and chopped

1 large yellow onion, minced

1 Scotch bonnet chile, cut in half

4 oz. green beans, chopped

3 medium carrots, peeled and cubed

2 chayote squash, cubed

1 red, yellow, and green bell pepper, stemmed, cubed

2 teaspoon light brown sugar

1 (14-oz.) can pigeon peas, rinsed and drained

Cooked white rice for serving

Black pepper, to taste

Chopped cilantro, for serving

Preparation

Boil the coconut milk in a Dutch oven and cook for 25 minutes on medium heat with occasional stirring. Stir in the chile, onion, tomatoes, garlic, thyme, scallions, and allspice. Then cook for 5 minutes. Stir in the peppers, chayote, carrots, and green beans. Then cook for 35 minutes with occasional stirring. Stir in the peas and the sugar and then cook for 5 minutes. Garnish with cilantro. Serve warm.

Rosemary-Jerk Lamb Chops

Preparation time: 15 minutes
Cook time: 14 minutes
Nutrition facts (per serving): 309 Cal (12g fat, 27g protein, 3g fiber)

Do you want to enjoy the famous jerk lamb chops? Then try this recipe and enjoy the best of all flavors in one single meal.

Ingredients (4 servings)

7 garlic cloves, peeled
2 scallions, chopped
1 medium yellow onion, chopped
1 sprig rosemary, stem removed
½ Scotch bonnet Chile stemmed and seeded
1 ½ tablespoon soy sauce
½ teaspoon ground allspice
2 lbs. lamb loin chops, cut 1 ½ inch thick, tails trimmed
Salt and black pepper, to taste

Preparation

Blend the allspice with the soy sauce, chile, rosemary, onion, scallions, and garlic in a food processor until smooth. Rub this marinade over the lamb chops, cover, and then refrigerate for 4 hours. Set a charcoal grill on high heat. Remove the pork from the marinade and season with black pepper and salt. Grill the lamb chops for 7 minute per side. Serve warm.

Plantain and Chickpea Curry

Preparation time: 15 minutes
Cook time: 12 minutes
Nutrition facts (per serving): 400 Cal (11g fat, 25g protein, 4g fiber)

The saucy plantain and chickpeas curry with brown rice will melt your heart with its great taste and excellent texture. Serve warm with cucumber salad on the side.

Ingredients (4 servings)

3 teaspoon vegetable oil

1 medium onion, diced

4 garlic cloves, chopped

3 teaspoon grated fresh ginger

1 teaspoon ground cumin

6 teaspoon dried mixed herbs

3 teaspoon chili powder

1 teaspoon all-purpose seasoning

4 ½ tablespoon curry powder

4 ½ cup water

7 oz. coconut milk

5 lbs. cans chickpeas, drained and rinsed

4 ripe plantain, peeled and sliced

1 Scotch bonnet pepper (Chili)

3 spring onions, sliced

1 teaspoon salt

3 teaspoon black pepper

5 oz. fresh callaloo or spinach

White rice, rice and peas, or roti, to serve

Preparation

Sauté the onion with ginger, garlic, and oil in a Dutch oven for 7 minutes. Stir in the curry powder, seasoning, chili powder, herbs, and cumin with a splash of water. Stir in the Scotch bonnet, plantain, chickpeas, coconut milk, water, and spring onion. Finally, cook for 5 minutes. Serve warm.

Jerk Pork Belly with Pea and Potato Mash

Preparation time: 10 minutes
Cook time: 3 hours 44 minutes
Nutrition facts (per serving): 386 Cal (13g fat, 29g protein, 2g fiber)

Let's have a rich and delicious combination of pork belly with pea and potato mash. Cook this meal at home and serve warm with some white rice.

Ingredients (4 servings)

1 pork belly, rind removed
1 tablespoon dry jerk seasoning
1 ¼ cup dry cider
2 cup chicken stock
1 onion, sliced
4 garlic cloves, sliced
4 fresh thyme sprigs
Pickapeppa or hot sauce, to serve
Pea and potato mash-up
1 ½ lbs. new potatoes, scraped or scrubbed
3 oz. olive oil
8 oz. shelled peas
Sea salt and black pepper, to taste

Preparation

At 350 degrees F, preheat your oven. Rub the pork belly with jerk seasoning. Place it in a cooking pan and sear until golden brown from both sides. Mix the stock and the cider in a suitable bowl. Spread the garlic, onion rings, and thyme over the pork belly and then pour the cider mixture on top. Cover with a foil sheet and roast for 3 hours. Increase the oven temperature to 425 degrees F, preheat your oven. Roast the pork for 25 minutes. Boil the potatoes with water in a cooking pot and then cook for 15 minutes until soft. Drain and mash the potatoes with olive oil and the seasoning in a suitable bowl. Boil the peas with water for 4 minutes and then add to the potatoes. Slice the roasted pork and serve with the mash-up. Enjoy.

Chicken A La Impress Me

Preparation time: 15 minutes
Cook time: 31 minutes
Nutrition facts (per serving): 209 Cal (8g fat, 31g protein, 4g fiber)

The Jamaican zucchini roll is not only delicious, but it also makes a healthy and loaded serving. You can eat it with white rice.

Ingredients (6 servings)

6 skinless, boneless chicken breasts

12 slices smoked ham

¾ cup Gruyere or similar hard yellow cheese, shredded

¼ cup carrots, julienned

¼ cup zucchini, julienned

1 tablespoon vegetable oil

Preparation

At 350 degrees F, preheat your oven. Place each chicken breast in between two plastic sheets and pound them with a mallet. Top each chicken with 2 ham slices, 2 tablespoon cheese, 1/6 carrots, and zucchini on top. Roll the chicken breasts and secure them with a toothpick. Sear the chicken rolls in a skillet greased with oil for 3 minutes per side. Transfer them to a 9x13 inches baking dish. Bake for 25 minutes and then serve warm.

Grilled Jerk Pork Tenderloin

Preparation time: 15 minutes
Cook time: 14 minutes
Nutrition facts (per serving): 248 Cal (11g fat, 27g protein, 0.2g fiber)

You can't really imagine a Jamaican menu without having these pork tenderloins on it. Now you can prepare them using this simple and quick recipe.

Ingredients (4 servings)
Marinade
2 habanero peppers, seeded
1 small onion, chopped
2 bunches of green onions, chopped
1 (1 inch) piece fresh ginger, peeled and sliced
3 garlic cloves, peeled
¼ cup apple cider
¼ cup white vinegar
3 tablespoon soy sauce
2 tablespoon olive oil
1½ tablespoon packed brown sugar
¾ teaspoon mustard seed
1 tablespoon salt
1 teaspoon black pepper
1 tablespoon dried thyme
1 tablespoon ground allspice
1 teaspoon ground nutmeg
½ teaspoon ground cinnamon
2½ pounds pork tenderloin, butterflied

Preparation

Blend the garlic, ginger, green onions, onion, and habanero peppers in a food processor. Add the sugar, olive oil, soy sauce, white vinegar, cider, cinnamon, nutmeg, allspice, thyme, black pepper, salt, and mustard seed and blend until smooth. Set the pork tenderloin in a shallow dish. Spread this mixture over the meat, cover and refrigerate for 8 hours. Set up a grill over medium-high heat and grease its grilling grate. Grill the pork tenderloin for 7 minutes per side. Slice and serve warm.

Grilled Boneless Pork with Mango Salsa

Preparation time: 10 minutes
Cook time: 70 minutes
Nutrition facts (per serving): 432 Cal (24g fat, 20g protein, 1.3g fiber)

Enjoy this pork with mango salad recipe on your Jamaican menu. This meal is loaded with meat and fiber-rich salsa.

Ingredients (6 servings)

3 pounds boneless pork loin

3 tablespoon dry Jamaican jerk seasoning

3 tablespoon olive oil

2 bananas, peeled and sliced

2 mangos, peeled and diced

1 jalapeno, seeds removed, chopped

½ red onion, diced

2 tablespoon lime juice

1 cup cilantro leaves, chopped

Preparation

At 350 degrees F, preheat your oven. Pat dry the pork and rub with 3 tablespoon Jerk seasoning. Cover and refrigerate the pork for 45 minutes. Rub the pork with olive oil, place on a baking sheet, and then bake for 45 minutes. Roast the bananas on a baking sheet for 25 minutes. Mix the caramelized bananas with the cilantro, lime juice, red onion, jalapeno, and mango in a suitable bowl. Serve with the pork chops.

Grilled Jerk Chicken with Mint Glaze

Preparation time: 10 minutes
Cook time: 16 minutes
Nutrition facts (per serving): 230 Cal (23g fat, 12g protein, 1g fiber)

Crispy and saucy, this jerk rubbed chicken recipe is so full of surprise. You'll love its amazing taste.

Ingredients (4 servings)
Jerk Rub
3 tablespoon ground coriander
3 tablespoon ground ginger
3 tablespoon light brown sugar
2 tablespoon onion powder
2 tablespoon garlic powder
2 tablespoon salt
2 tablespoon habanero powder
1 tablespoon dry thyme
2 teaspoon coarse black pepper
2 teaspoon ground cinnamon
2 teaspoon ground allspice
2 teaspoon ground cloves

Habanero-Mint Glaze
1 ½ cups red wine vinegar
1 ½ cups white wine vinegar
3 cups sugar
1 habanero chile, chopped
½ cup fresh mint leaves, chopped
Salt, to taste

Chicken

2 pounds chicken thighs, bone-in

Canola oil

Preparation

Mix the vinegar with the sugar in a medium saucepan and cook over medium-high heat until reduced to half. Blend this mixture with the mint habanero and salt in a blender until smooth. Set up the grill over medium heat. Rub the chicken with the jerk rub and oil. Grill the chicken for 4 minutes per side. Brush the chicken with the mint glaze and cook for 8 more minutes. Serve warm.

Desserts

Jamaican Grater Cake

Preparation time: 15 minutes
Nutrition facts (per serving): 360 Cal (14g fat, 8g protein, 1g fiber)

This Jamaican grater cake recipe gives you an easy way to enjoy a fancy dessert, and this recipe will let you cook a delicious serving in no time.

Ingredients (6 servings)

2 cups water
1 ½ cups sugar
½ inch ginger root
2 cups coconut, grated
⅛ teaspoon salt
⅛ teaspoon vanilla
½ teaspoon food color

Preparation

Grate the coconut flesh in a food processor. Grease a cake pan with oil. Mix the ginger, water, and sugar in a saucepan and cook with stirring until the sugar is caramelized. Remove the sugar from the heat and add the salt and the coconut. Mix well and cook on medium-low heat until the mixture is reduced. Add the vanilla and mix until the mixture leaves the sides of the pan. Spread ⅔ of this mixture in the prepared pan. Mix the remaining batter with food color and spread on top of the white layer. Leave the layers for 30 minutes to harden. Cut in bars and serve.

Jamaican Upside-Down Cake

Preparation time: 10 minutes
Cook time: 60 minutes
Nutrition facts (per serving): 319 Cal (10g fat, 5g protein, 4g fiber)

Count on this upside-down cake to make your dessert menu extra special and surprise your loved one with the ultimate flavors.

Ingredients (6 servings)
9 tablespoons unsalted butter
1 ½ cups packed dark-brown sugar
1 pineapple, peeled, cored, and sliced
1 can (13.5 ounces) coconut milk
3 large eggs, beaten
1 tablespoon grated lime zest
2 tablespoons lime juice
2 teaspoons vanilla extract
3 cups all-purpose flour
1 tablespoon baking powder
2 teaspoons ground allspice
1 teaspoon salt

Preparation
At 350 degrees F, preheat your oven. Grease a 9-inch round baking pan with melted butter and top it with ½ cup sugar and pineapple slices in a single layer. Mix the rest of the ingredients in a mixer until smooth and pour over the pineapples in the baking pan. Spread it evenly and bake for 1 hour in the oven. Allow the cake to cool and then flip it over the serving plate. Serve.

Jamaican Rum Cake

Preparation time: 15 minutes
Cook time: 73 minutes
Nutrition facts (per serving): 455 Cal (6g fat, 11g protein, 3g fiber)

Here's a delicious and savory combination of rum butter syrup with rum cake. All the right ingredients are mixed in a perfect balance to give you a great dessert.

Ingredients (6 servings)
Cake
2 ¼ cups flour
¼ cup corn starch
3 teaspoon baking powder
½ teaspoon salt
1 ¼ cups sugar
½ cup soft butter
¼ cup canola oil
½ cup evaporated milk
4 eggs
1 tablespoon pure vanilla extract
⅓ cup rum

Rum butter syrup
¼ cup butter
½ cup sugar
¼ cup water
¾ cup rum

½ teaspoon vanilla extract

Preparations

At 325 degrees F, preheat your oven. Grease a Bundt pan with oil. Mix the flour with sugar, butter, salt, oil, baking powder, and cornstarch at low speed until the mixture gets crumbly. Stir in the eggs and milk and then mix well. Add the vanilla and the rum and then mix until smooth. Spread this prepared batter in the Bundt pan and bake for 65 minutes. Allow the cake to cool. Meanwhile, boil the sugar, water, and butter in a pan for 8 minutes. Add vanilla and rum then remove from the heat. Mix well and pour the syrup over the cake. Cover and refrigerate the cake overnight. Slice and serve.

Coconut Drops

Preparation time: 10 minutes
Cook time: 60 minutes
Nutrition facts (per serving): 223 Cal (16g fat, 9g protein, 2g fiber)

Have you ever tried the Jamaican coconut drops? Well, here's a recipe to cook them by yourself with easy-to-follow ingredients.

Ingredients (12 servings)

2 cups diced coconut

1 teaspoon vanilla

1 lb. brown sugar

1 pinch salt

1 teaspoon powdered ginger

½ cup water

Preparation

Cut the coconut into ¼ inch pieces and rinse with cold water. Add the coconut, water, and the rest of the ingredients to a saucepan and cook for 40 minutes with occasional stirring. Divide the coconut mixture onto a greased baking sheet spoon by spoon. Allow the coconut drops to cool for 20 minutes. Serve.

Hummingbird Cake

Preparation time: 15 minutes
Cook time: 30 minutes
Nutrition facts (per serving): 197 Cal (6g fat, 1g protein, 4g fiber)

If you haven't tried Jamaican hummingbird cake before, then here comes a simple and easy to cook recipe that you can recreate at home in no time with minimum efforts.

Ingredients (6 servings)
Cake
3 cups all-purpose flour
2 cups granulated sugar
1 teaspoon ground cinnamon
1 teaspoon baking soda
1 teaspoon salt
3 large eggs beaten
1 ¼ cup vegetable oil
2 teaspoon vanilla extract
8 oz. crushed pineapple with juice
1 ¾ cup ripe mashed bananas
1 cup pecans, chopped

Cream Cheese Frosting
1 cup unsalted butter
8 oz. cream cheese
3 ½ cups confectioner's sugar
1 pinch of salt

2 teaspoon pineapple juice

2 teaspoon vanilla extract

¼ cup pecans, chopped

Preparation

At 350 degrees F, preheat your oven. Grease 2- 9 inches round baking pans with cooking spray and layer them with parchment paper. Mix the flour with salt, baking soda, cinnamon, and sugar in a suitable bowl. Beat in the eggs, mashed bananas, pineapple and its juice, vanilla, and oil and then mix evenly. Divide the batter into the baking pan and bake for 30 minutes. Allow them to cool for 15 minutes. Beat the cream cheese with the butter in a mixer until fluffy. Slowly add the sugar and continue the mixture. Stir in the vanilla and the pineapple juice and mix. Cut each cake horizontally into two layers. Place one cake layer at the bottom, top it with ¼ frosting, and then place another layer on top. Add ¼ frosting on top and repeat the layers with the remaining cakes and frosting. Garnish with pecans and serve.

Jamaican Ginger Cake

Preparation time: 15 minutes
Cook time: 45 minutes
Nutrition facts (per serving): 265 Cal (12g fat, 5g protein, 1g fiber)

The famous ginger cake is here to make your Jamaican cuisine extra special. Serve it along with other candies and cookies.

Ingredients (8 servings)

3 cups of flour
1 cup of butter
1 cup of coconut sugar
½ cup of blackstrap molasses
1 cup of hot water
2 large eggs
1 teaspoon of baking soda
1 teaspoon of baking powder
2 teaspoon of ground ginger
1 tablespoon of fresh ginger grated
1 teaspoon of ground cinnamon
1 teaspoon of ground nutmeg
½ teaspoon of ground pimento allspice
1 teaspoon vanilla essence
¼ teaspoon Himalayan pink salt

Preparation

At 360 degrees F, preheat your oven. Layer two loaf pans with wax paper. Mix the flour with pink salt, baking soda, pimento, nutmeg, and cinnamon in a suitable bowl. Beat the butter with the coconut sugar in a mixer until creamy. Beat in the eggs, vanilla extract, and ginger. Beat for 2 minutes. Mix the molasses with 1 cup hot water in a suitable bowl and mix until it melts. Pour half of the molasses and half of the flour mixture into the mixer. Mix evenly on medium speed and then add the remaining molasses and the flour mixture. Mix well for 2 minutes and then divide the batter into the loaf pans. Bake the cakes for 40-45 minutes. Allow them to cool and then slice to serve.

Jamaican Christmas Cake

Preparation time: 10 minutes
Cook time: 45 minutes
Nutrition facts (per serving): 691 Cal (51g fat, 3.3g protein, 2g fiber)

Have you ever tried the Jamaican Christmas cake? If not, then here comes a recipe that will help you cook the finest cake in no time.

Ingredients (8 servings)

16 oz. dark brown sugar

16 oz. unsalted butter

12 large eggs

2 tablespoon vanilla

2 tablespoon rose water

2 tablespoon mixed essence

6 oz. all-purpose flour, sifted

6 oz. breadcrumbs plain

1 tablespoon salt

2 tablespoon baking powder

2 tablespoon cinnamon

2 tablespoon ginger grounded

1 tablespoon mixed spice

1 tablespoon nutmeg grounded

½ tablespoon cloves grounded

½ cup raisins dried

½ cup currants dried

½ cup cranberries dried

½ cup prunes, chopped and pitted

½ cup dates, chopped and dried

½ cup candied cherries

½ cup candied mixed peel

2 cups red port wine

1 cup Jamaican white rum

2 tablespoon molasses

4 tablespoon browning

1 tablespoon baking soda

2 tablespoon almond flavor

Preparation

Beat the brown sugar with the butter in a mixing bowl with an electric mixer. Beat in the eggs and mix until creamy. Stir in the almond flavor, mixed essence, rose water, and vanilla and then mix well. Mix the flour with all other dry ingredients in a suitable bowl and then add to the eggs mixture while mixing gently. Heat 1 ¾ cup port wine with ¾ of the white rum, currants, raisins, prunes, cranberries, cherries, dates, and candied peel in a saucepan over low heat and cook until the liquid is evaporated. Add the fruit mixture to the batter and mix evenly. Stir in the browning and the molasses and mix again. Grease 2- 8 inches baking pans with butter and divide the prepared batter in them. Bake them for 45 minutes at 350 degrees F. Allow the cake to cool and mix ¼ cup port wine, and ⅛ cup white rum in a suitable bowl. Pour this liquid over the cake. Leave it for 5 minutes, slice, and serve.

Jamaican Pineapple Cake

Preparation time: 15 minutes
Cook time: 60 minutes
Nutrition facts (per serving): 396 Cal (23g fat, 8g protein, 0g fiber)

If you haven't tried the delicious Jamaican cake before, then here comes a simple and easy cook this recipe that you can recreate at home in no time with minimum efforts.

Ingredients (8 servings)

2 cups white sugar

1 ½ cups vegetable oil

1 ½ cups pecans, chopped

3 cups all-purpose flour

2 bananas, peeled and diced

3 eggs

1 (20 oz.) can crush pineapple with juice

1 teaspoon vanilla extract

1 teaspoon salt

1 teaspoon baking soda

Preparation

Mix all the dry and wet ingredients together in a mixing bowl and then fold in the bananas. Mix and spread the batter into a 13x9 inches baking pan. Bake this batter for 60 minutes at 350 degrees F. Once done, allow it to cool and serve.

Jamaican Coconut Toto

Preparation time: 5 minutes
Cook time: 30 minutes
Nutrition facts (per serving): 248 Cal (13g fat, 9g protein, 6g fiber)

These coconut totos make an excellent dessert serving! They're loved by all, young and adult, due to the delicious mix of evaporated milk and grated coconut.

Ingredients (6 servings)

¼ cup butter

3 cups flour

1 cup sugar

2 eggs

1 teaspoon vanilla

3 teaspoons baking powder

1 teaspoon cinnamon

1 teaspoon salt

¼ teaspoon nutmeg

2 cups grated coconut

1 cup evaporated milk

Preparation

Beat the butter with the sugar in a mixing bowl until creamy. Stir in the vanilla and the eggs. Then beat for 2 minutes. Add the cinnamon, baking powder, flour, and nutmeg. Mix well and then pour in the evaporated milk. Mix until smooth. Spread this prepared batter into an 8x12 inches greased baking pan. Bake it for 30 minutes at 400 degrees F. Serve.

Jamaican Mango Cheesecake

Preparation time: 15 minutes
Cook time: 2 hours 50 minutes
Nutrition facts (per serving): 384 Cal (19g fat, 5g protein, 1.4g fiber)

Try this mango cheesecake dessert and enjoy the best of the savory flavors. The recipe is simple and gives you lots of nutrients in one place.

Ingredients (8 servings)
Crust
1 cup cracker crumbs

1 cup sugar

1 teaspoon Jamaican cinnamon

½ cup melted butter

½ teaspoon salt

¼ cup Jamaican peanuts, chopped

Filling
2 ½ cups Jamaican mango puree

2 cups sour cream

2 tablespoon brown sugar

2 teaspoon vanilla

3 eggs

3 packages (8 oz.) cream cheese, softened

Zest of ½ Jamaican orange

Preparation

At 350 degrees F, preheat your oven. Mix all the crust ingredients in a suitable bowl and spread the crust evenly in a springform pan. Beat the sour cream with cream cheese and the rest of the ingredients in a bowl with an electric mixture. Pour the filling into the crust, and then place the pan in a roasting sheet with some water in it. Bake the cheesecake for 2 ½ hours. Increase the temperature to 400 degrees F and continue baking for 20 minutes. Allow the cake to cool, slice, and serve.

Fruit Salad

Preparation time: 10 minutes
Cook time: 5 minutes
Nutrition facts (per serving): 207 Cal (8g fat, 13g protein, 1g fiber)

This fruit salad makes up a great side for the table, and you can serve it with delicious and healthy entrees as well.

Ingredients (4 servings)
2 bananas
Lemon juice from 1 lemon
2 oranges
1 grapefruit
7 oz. seedless cherries
1 oz. hazelnuts
½ cup of melon pieces, cubed
2 kiwis, sliced
1 cup raspberries and blue berries

Dressing
2 tablespoons of Greek yogurt
Lemon juice from ½ lemon
1 teaspoon brandy
1 teaspoon of honey

Preparation

Toast the nuts in a pan until golden and then crush them in a food processor. Mix the rest of the dressing ingredients in a salad bowl and toss in all the fruits. Garnish with nuts. Serve.

Drinks

Jamaican Rum Punch

Preparation time: 15 minutes
Nutrition facts (per serving): 254 Cal (0.9g fat, 1.6g protein, 7g fiber)

The Jamaican rum punch is famous for its amazing blend of pineapple juice, orange juice, and grenadine syrup.

Ingredients (6 servings)
2 ½ cups pineapple juice
2 ½ cups orange juice
1 cup 151 proof rum
½ cup dark rum
¼ cup coconut-flavored rum
¼ cup fresh lime juice
3 tablespoon grenadine syrup
1 orange, sliced
1 lime, sliced
1 lemon, sliced

Preparation
Mix the pineapple, lime, and orange juice with the rums and the grenadine syrup in a punch bowl. Garnish with orange, lime, and lemon slices and then serves.

Jamaican Breeze Cocktail

Preparation time: 5 minutes
Nutrition facts (per serving): 122 Cal (13g fat, 3g protein, 1g fiber)

The Jamaican breeze cocktail drink is famous for its blend of pineapple juice and angostura bitters. You can prep this drink easily at home with this basic recipe.

Ingredients (1 serving)

1-piece fresh ginger, peeled
1 ½ ounces Appleton Estate Reserve Rum
2 ounces pineapple juice
½-ounce simple syrup
1 dash Angostura bitters
1 Lime wheel to garnish

Preparation

Shake the run with the rest of the ingredients in a cocktail shaker and pour into a glass with ice. Garnish with lime and serve.

White Jamaican Cocktail

Preparation time: 5 minutes
Nutrition facts (per serving): 445 Cal (8g fat, 1g protein, 1.4g fiber)

Have this white Jamaica drink and enjoy the best of the coconut rum's flavors in this drink. Serve it chilled for the best taste.

Ingredients (2 servings)
Crushed ice
1 ½ oz. vanilla vodka
1 ½ oz. coconut rum
1 ½ oz. Coffee liqueur
¾ oz. heavy whipping cream

Preparation
Fill a ¾ of a shaker with ice, add vodka, coconut rum, coffee liqueur, and cream. Cover and shake for 15 seconds. Strain the drink into a glass and serve.

Jamaican Sorrel Drink

Preparation time: 5 minutes
Cook time: 40 minutes
Nutrition facts (per serving): 120 Cal (0g fat, 0.1g protein, 1g fiber)

Here's a special Jamaican hibiscus drink made from dried hibiscus and ginger, so it's super refreshing.

Ingredients (6 servings)

2 cups dried hibiscus

2 inches ginger, sliced

1 orange, peel

2 cinnamon sticks

6 cups water

1 cup sugar

Preparation

Add the hibiscus and the rest of the ingredients to a saucepan and cook for 40 minutes on a simmer. Strain and allow the drink to cool. Serve chilled with ice.

Jamaican Mule

Preparation time: 5 minutes
Nutrition facts (per serving): 112 Cal (0g fat, 0.1g protein, 1.3g fiber)

Made from ginger beer, rum, and lime juice, this beverage is a refreshing addition to the Jamaican cocktail menu.

Ingredients (2 servings)

¼ cup Appleton Estate Reserve Rum

⅔ cup ginger beer

1 squeeze of lime

1 lime wedge

Cubed ice

Preparation

Shake the rum with the ginger beer and the lime juice in a shaker. Pour into a glass filled with ice. Garnish with a lime wedge. Serve.

Jamaican Carrot Juice

Preparation time: 5 minutes
Cook time: 35 minutes
Nutrition facts (per serving): 116 Cal (0g fat, 0.1g protein, 0 g fiber)

This refreshing sweet carrot juice is always a delight to serve at parties. Now you can make it easily at home by using the following simple ingredients.

Ingredients (4 servings)
2 pounds carrots, chopped
4 cups water
1 can condensed milk
½ teaspoon nutmeg
1 teaspoon vanilla extract
½ teaspoon fresh ginger
1 can coconut milk
⅓ cup coconut sugar

Preparation
Boil the coconut milk with the sugar in a medium saucepan. Reduce its heat and cook for 35 minutes on medium heat. Allow it to cool. Puree the carrots with 3 cups water. Strain the carrot juice by passing through a cheesecloth. Squeeze the cloth tightly to extract all the juice. Rinse the blender and blend the carrot juice, the rest of the milk, and the remainder of the ingredients in it. Serve.

Old Jamaican

Preparation time: 5 minutes
Nutrition facts (per serving): 161 Cal (0g fat, 0g protein, 1g fiber)

This old Jamaican cocktail is a great beverage to serve at any time. It delivers a unique blend of rum, lime juice, and simple syrup.

Ingredients (4 servings)
1 sprig of fresh mint
1 oz. lime juice
1 ½ oz. Appleton Estate Reserve Rum
¾ oz. pure cane simple syrup
1 dash Angostura bitters
Champagne, to top
Garnish
Mint sprig

Preparation
Muddle the lime juice and the mint in a cocktail shaker. Add the bitters, simple syrup and rum. Next, shake well. Pour into a highball glass and add ice. Pour champagne on top. Garnish with mint and serve.

If you liked Jamaican recipes, discover to how cook DELICIOUS recipes from **Balkan** countries!

Within these pages, you'll learn 35 authentic recipes from a Balkan cook. These aren't ordinary recipes you'd find on the Internet, but recipes that were closely guarded by our Balkan mothers and passed down from generation to generation.

Main Dishes, Appetizers, and Desserts included!

If you want to learn how to make Croatian green peas stew, and 32 other authentic Balkan recipes, then start with our book!

Order at www.balkanfood.org/cook-books/ for only $2,99

Maybe Hungarian cuisine?

Order at www.balkanfood.org/cook-books/ for only $2,99

If you're a **Mediterranean** dieter who wants to know the secrets of the Mediterranean diet, dieting, and cooking, then you're about to discover how to master cooking meals on a Mediterranean diet right now!

In fact, if you want to know how to make Mediterranean food, then this new e-book - "The 30-minute Mediterranean diet" - gives you the answers to many important questions and challenges every Mediterranean dieter faces, including:

- How can I succeed with a Mediterranean diet?
- What kind of recipes can I make?
- What are the key principles to this type of diet?
- What are the suggested weekly menus for this diet?
- Are there any cheat items I can make?

... and more!

If you're serious about cooking meals on a Mediterranean diet and you really want to know how to make Mediterranean food, then you need to grab a copy of "The 30-minute Mediterranean diet" right now.

Prepare **111 recipes with several ingredients in less than 30 minutes**!

Order at www.balkanfood.org/cook-books/ for only $2,99

What could be better than a home-cooked meal? Maybe only a **Greek** homemade meal.

Do not get discouraged if you have no Greek roots or friends. Now you can make a Greek food feast in your kitchen.

This ultimate Greek cookbook offers you 111 best dishes of this cuisine! From more famous gyros to more exotic *Kota Kapama* this cookbook keeps it easy and affordable.

All the ingredients necessary are wholesome and widely accessible. The author's picks are as flavorful as they are healthy. The dishes described in this cookbook are "what Greek mothers have made for decades."

Full of well-balanced and nutritious meals, this handy cookbook includes many vegan options. Discover a plethora of benefits of Mediterranean cuisine, and you may fall in love with cooking at home.

Inspired by a real food lover, this collection of delicious recipes will taste buds utterly satisfied.

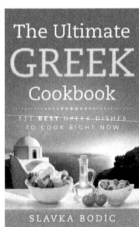

Order at www.balkanfood.org/cook-books/ for only $2,99

Maybe some Swedish meatballs ?

Maybe to try exotic **Syrian** cuisine?

From succulent *sarma*, soups, warm and cold salads to delectable desserts, the plethora of flavors will satisfy the most jaded foodie. Have a taste of a new culture with this **traditional Syrian cookbook**.

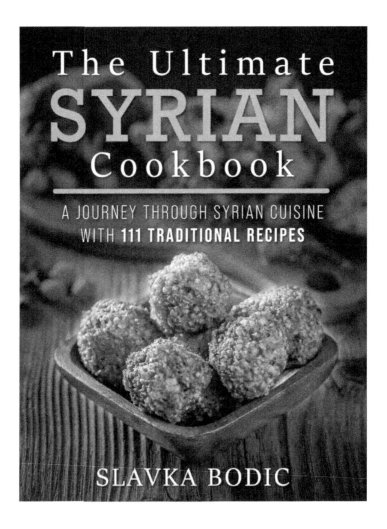

Order at www.balkanfood.org/cook-books/ for only $2,99

Maybe **Polish** cuisine?

Order at www.balkanfood.org/cook-books/ for only $2,99

Or **Peruvian**?

Order at www.balkanfood.org/cook-books/ for only $2,99

ONE LAST THING

If you enjoyed this book or found it useful, I'd be very grateful if you could find the time to post a short review on Amazon. Your support really does make a difference and I read all the reviews personally, so I can get your feedback and make this book even better.

Thanks again for your support!

Please send me your feedback at

www.balkanfood.org

Printed in Great Britain
by Amazon